Jonah
Pride & Prejudice

Jonah
Pride & Prejudice

Kieran Beville

ISPCK
2010

Jonah: Pride & Prejudice — Published by the Rev. Dr. Ashish Amos of the Indian Society for Promoting Christian Knowledge (ISPCK), Post Box 1585, 1654, Madarsa Road, Kashmere Gate, Delhi - 110006.

© Kieran Beville 2010

ISBN :

Laser typeset at **ISPCK**, Post Box 1585, 1654, Madarsa Road, Kashmere Gate, Delhi - 110006.
Tel : 23866323, 23866322
e-mail : ashish@ispck.org.in   ella@ispck.org.in
website : www.ispck.org.in

'For the gifts and the calling
of God are irrevocable'
(Romans 11: 29)

Contents

Preface

This book emerged from as a series of sermons which were subsequently adapted for publication. It focuses primarily on the application of the message of *Jonah* and as such is an exhortation to the contemporary church.

There are a few quotations without the full credits one might expect in a written work. The reason for this is that in an oral presentation, in the context of a regular preaching ministry, one would credit the author but not, necessarily, the publication details. So an author may be credited in the text without further reference details in footnotes or endnotes.

In order to distinguish between Jonah, the man and *Jonah*, the book, the latter is italicised wherever it is mentioned. Other books of the *Bible* (and their abbreviated form in parenthesis) are not italicised. I trust this will not appear inconsistent.

I want to express my sincere thanks to my wife, Ber, for reading the manuscript and for her helpful comments and consistent support and encouragement. I also acknowledge the help of Pastor Philip Brown for his appraisal of the manuscript and his constructive suggestions.

I hope the reader of the ensuing pages will come to a fuller appreciation of the gracious and merciful nature of God. It would please me immensely if this book worked for the glory of God and the good of His children; especially if it assists in the process of spiritual transformation by the renewing of our minds (Rom.12:12).

Finally, if this work contributes to stimulating evangelistic endeavour I will be greatly gratified.

Introduction

Doctrine In Drama

The book of *Jonah* is a brief but fascinating story. Its vivid and dramatic narrative engages the emotions and imaginations of its readers. As such it has all the elements of good drama. In this Old Testament prophetic book, however, we see beyond its exciting and thrilling elements to an astonishing account of God's dealings with the prophet. In this sense it is biographical because it tells something of the life and ministry of Jonah. We are given only a summary of the substance of his preaching because God wants us to get hold of something else. When we come to see that this book provides an amazing insight into the heart of God then we have begun to catch a glimpse is its central and glorious theme. Thus it is the largeness of the heart of God that provides us with the central theme of the book. It is with this key that we unlock the meaning of *Jonah* and hear its recurring overtures of grace. There is doctrine in this drama and so it will be profitable to reflect on its themes and teaching.

Main theme

The thematic thrust of the book is about the magnitude of the heart of God; a heart that is larger than the borders of Israel. His affection extends beyond the boundaries of the covenant nation. He is not a bigoted, narrow-hearted, tribal God. He is merciful to the undeserving.

The heart of Jonah is portrayed in contrast, not only with the heart of God, but also contrasted with the pagan people of Nineveh (including their king), and the pagan sailors. He typified a people who were smug, insular, inward looking and self-centred.

Importantly, it is also a book that has a message for today. Rooted in the actual events of a specific time and place it nevertheless has a timeless and timely message. We cannot leave *Jonah* in the 'then and there' because that would be a flawed approach to a biblical understanding of Scripture. We are concerned to investigate elements of the 'then and there' but only insofar as they lay a foundation for our understanding of how *Jonah* relates to the 'here and now'. In doing this we are taking God at His Word. For the Word of God tells us that, 'All Scripture *is* given by inspiration of God, and *is* profitable for doctrine, for reproof, for correction, for instruction in righteousness' (2 Tim.3:16). We will, therefore, investigate this Old Testament book as a text that is divinely inspired and authored by God. Because we accept its authoritative rule in all matters of faith and practice we will ask, what does it teach us? Where does it rebuke us? How can it correct us? In what ways can it contribute to our training in righteousness?

Most Christians are very familiar with the narrative details of *Jonah*. This has both advantages and disadvantages. It is beneficial to have previous acquaintance with the facts of the narrative before engaging in a more in-depth study of the book. Nevertheless it may not, necessarily, be a good thing to be too familiar with the story if such familiarity hinders a fresh investigation that seeks to emphasise its contemporary application. *Jonah* is not just a story with a moral lesson tacked on. We need to overcome this common misunderstanding of the book if we are to open up its message.

Perhaps the problem begins with the way the book is presented to children. It is a favourite with the very young, and is often represented in pictorial *Bibles*. It is a story that lends itself well to illustration because it evokes lucid scenes in the mind's eye. Most Christian parents delight in telling their enraptured children this tale, and their children in turn love the adventure of this book and never tire of its sensational elements. But *Jonah* is not merely a literary creation like *Pinocchio[1]*. It is not just a story that is designed to illustrate a moral or spiritual lesson. It is neither fable nor parable.

Those who were brought up with Christian parents were probably introduced to it in childhood, either at home or in Sunday-School class. However, that very association with childhood can characterise one's approach to the text. There is a difference between a *child-like* receptivity to Scripture and a *childish* understanding of the Word. The former is to be commended as a way of thinking that is open to learning, innocent, pure, uncomplicated and trusting whereas the latter is to be condemned as immature, irresponsible, foolish and infantile. Therefore a *childlike* way of thinking will always prove beneficial in reading any biblical text, but a *childish* mindset will be a barrier to understanding.

A fable is a fictional story, especially if it has a supernatural dimension. Such moral tales often have animals as characters[2] and in this we see certain parallels between *Pinocchio* and the prophetic book. Jonah was swallowed by 'a great fish' and Pinocchio was swallowed by a whale. Both stories have supernatural elements. When we become adults we do not always leave behind the impressions of our formative years. Let us look beyond the adventure story to the moral lesson but let us not stop there.

---

[1] This is the title of Carlo Lorenzini's book, *Pinocchio*, about the childlike puppet whose adventures delight children around the world. It was further popularised by Walt Disney, the famous film producer and pioneer of animated films, in his much loved cartoon film of the same name.

[2] Like, *The Musicians of Bremen*, for example.

Rather let us look into the very heart of God and in so doing develop a greater understanding and appreciation of Him and discover in ourselves the need to be transformed more and more into His likeness.

Undoubtedly, reading *Jonah* will be profitable for correcting wrong attitudes and admonishing obedience to God. Unquestionably, it is a story with a supernatural dimension that features a creature of the sea. But the 'great fish' is not in any sense anthropomorphic.[3]

A parable is a story (not necessarily about real people and events) that illustrates some religious truth. Jesus used this valuable method of instruction because truth embodied in a story is accessible to all people irrespective of their level of education or intellectual ability. Parables, however, are not merely an interesting method of presenting important principles. They enlighten and persuade in a unique and compelling way. The parable uses familiar imagery in such a way that it brings new and unfamiliar insights. In this way it is an engaging form of communication. The parable, therefore, has its place in Scripture and functions perfectly well wherever it is used. But *Jonah* is not a parable and so we must be careful not to treat it as such. We will therefore look at the obvious truths in the book; truths that are relevant in context and contemporary application. So *Jonah* is not allegorical, in the sense that moral truth is merely symbolically represented in its pages. When Jesus (in Matthew and Luke) authenticates the story of *Jonah*, He is not referring to a parable but to historical fact. Thus he says:

> "An evil and adulterous generation seeks after a sign, and no sign will be given to it except the sign of the prophet Jonah. For as Jonah was three days and three nights in the belly of

---

[3] Anthropomorphism is the attribution of human characteristics to an animal, such as speech, intelligence and so on. The creature of the deep is not presented in that way in *Jonah*.

the great fish, so will the Son of Man be three days and three nights in the heart of the earth. The men of Nineveh will rise up in the judgment with this generation and condemn it, because they repented at the preaching of Jonah; and indeed a greater than Jonah *is* here" (Mt. 12: 39-41).

The words of Jesus are clear. He believed in the historical reality that Jonah spent three days and three nights in the belly of the great fish. Not only that but he linked that incident to the historical reality of His bodily resurrection. If we discard one then we must, logically, discount the other also! If we allegorise *Jonah* then by implication we must do likewise with the physical resurrection, which is fundamental to the Christian faith.

The Story

The narrative is straightforward and neatly divided into chapters. It may be summarised as follows.

In chapter 1, the prophet is commissioned by God to go to the great Assyrian city, Nineveh and proclaim its impending destruction because its wickedness offends God. Jonah does not want to fulfil this commission because Nineveh might repent and be spared only to fulfil its predicted role in the chastisement of Israel. He flees to Joppa and embarks on a journey to Tarshish which is in the opposite direction. A fierce storm engulfs the ship, and in spite of the captain's and the crew's best efforts the vessel is in imminent danger of breaking up. Lots are cast, and Jonah acknowledges that it is his presence on board that is causing the storm. At his suggestion he is thrown overboard and the storm subsides. God prepared a great fish to swallow Jonah.

In chapter 2, Jonah is trapped inside the stomach of this creature for three days and nights. He prays from within the fish. His prayer is a testimony of thanksgiving to God with elements of petitioning and promising. It is conveyed in a style which suggests that the prophet is reporting his experience to others. It reads very much like a testimony to God's deliverance and grace which presents profound truths as convictions rediscovered, reinforced and refined in a time of affliction. Perhaps it is a record of how he reported his experience to the Ninevites. In this chapter Jonah resolves to obey God. The tremendous truths that are stated seem to stand out in the text as the essence of distilled wisdom. Here are conclusions formed in the crucible of experience. Verse 8, for example, says, "Those who cling to worthless idols forfeit the grace that could be theirs". Verse 10 says "Salvation is of the LORD." In these statements we find the glorious gospel of grace. The prophet is disgorged onto the shore.

In chapter 3, Jonah is graciously re-commissioned by God but this time his response is different. He obeys the command to go to Nineveh and prophesy against the city. The inhabitants of the city repent and judgement is averted. In this we are presented with a picture of the profound nature of God's grace.

In chapter 4, we come to see that this is not the outcome that Jonah desired and he becomes angry. Obviously he had been hoping that catastrophe would befall the Assyrian heathen as he sat outside the city and awaited its destruction. A plant grew overnight which provided him with welcome shelter from the intense heat of the day but this in turn was destroyed by a worm. Jonah is greatly disappointed at the destruction of the plant. Then God speaks to him and it is these concluding words of the book that reinforce to us the true nature of the heart of God:

> But the LORD said, "You have had pity on the plant for which you have not laboured, nor made it grow, which came up in a night and perished in a night. And should I not pity Nineveh, that great city, in which are more than one hundred and twenty thousand persons who cannot discern between their right hand and their left—and much livestock?"

Background

Jonah was a prophet of God during the reign of Jeroboam II, the monarch of the Northern Kingdom of Israel in the eighth century B. C. His call from God to go to Nineveh was unusual, not because of the message he was to bring, but because of the people to whom he was to carry it. They were Gentiles. In fact Jonah was the first Hebrew prophet to be sent to a Gentile population. Jonah was the successor to Elijah and Elisha and was probably acquainted with them both and he was the link between them and Hosea, Amos and Isaiah. The fact that Jonah was a historical character is important and once again we emphasise that the tendency to think of this book as a parable needs correction.

This was a very significant and important assignment from God. It represented a new departure in His dealings with humanity and challenged Jonah's theology. This was without precedent. The prophet was asked to leave the precincts of Israel and go right to the heart of heathendom and proclaim that their wickedness was offensive to God. God did a new thing.

The Assyrian Empire was an ancient kingdom on the Upper Tigris (now Northern Iraq), where the Assyrians (named after their god Ashur) settled in about 2500 B.C.[4] The Assyrians were notorious pagans who were infamous for their savage cruelties. One of these grim cruelties was flaying people alive! In his proclamation the king of Nineveh identifies 'violence' as an evil that needs to be set aside. Thus we read: 'But let man and beast be covered with

---

[4] They came under the influence of Babylon. Ashur-uballit I (c. 1365 – c.1330) who laid the foundations of the Empire, which was extended by Tiglath-pileser I (1120–1074), who conquered the city of Babylon. A new era of conquest was begun by Ashurnasirpal II (883–859). The Assyrian Empire was extended to Syria and Palestine under Shalmaneser III (858–824) and Assyrian power reached its height under Tiglath-pileser III (745–727). Nineveh, the capital, fell to Media and Babylon in 612.

sackcloth, and cry mightily to God; yes, let every one turn from his evil way and from the violence that is in his hands' (3:8). The barbarous people of that city repented at the message of impending doom. So Nineveh was the capital city of Assyria at the time of Jonah's ministry. God therefore, gave him an assignment of major proportions.

The central purpose of the book is to show the largeness of the heart of God. God's people needed to understand that His heart is gracious and that His love extended beyond the borders of Israel. Certainly God had a special love for Israel, but He was not a tribal God whose love was restricted to Israel. God's people had become bigoted and their shrivelled hearts did not reflect the expansive love of God. The meagreness of their love misrepresented the magnitude of God's mercy. God had entered covenant relationship with a man (Abram) and that covenant embraced his family, clan, tribe and the other tribes of Israel and Judah. But the promise was that through Abraham *all nations* would be blessed. This was ultimately fulfilled in Christ but it was never intended that covenant blessing would not commence until Gentiles were converted to Christ.

God's Inclusive Plans

God's plan of redemption always included individuals outside of Israel. We see this with Rahab the heathen harlot who was grafted in to God's purposes. It is worth developing this point because it is helpful to our understanding of both the heart of God and the heart of Jonah.

Rahab lived in a house built into the walls of Jericho. The two spies sent by Joshua lodged there with her. When this became known it was reported to the King of Jericho who sent word to Rahab to turn over these enemies of Jericho. She disobeyed the king and concealed them under drying stalks of flax on the roof. When the city of Jericho and all its inhabitants was destroyed Rahab, her parents, possessions and relatives were spared. Thereafter she lived in Israel and is mentioned in three of the New Testament books. In Matthew she is listed in the genealogy of Jesus: 'Salmon begot Boaz by Rahab, Boaz begot Obed by Ruth, Obed begot Jesse' (1: 5). She was woven into God's grand scheme. In Hebrews we are told that it was, 'By faith the harlot Rahab did not perish with those who did not believe, when she had received the spies with peace' (11: 31). In this chapter she, once a heathen prostitute, is listed with the great patriarchs and heroes of faith. But we should also bear in mind that Abraham too was once a pagan and was also a flawed character that lied to a king, claiming that Sarah, was his sister (not his wife). He did this because he feared what the king might do to him in order to be with Sarah. This shows Abraham to be both a liar and a coward. This incident took place after he was called by God! We mention this because the notion that the Christian life is one of sinless perfection needs to be dispelled.

In James also Rahab is identified along with Abraham, 'Likewise, was not Rahab the harlot also justified by works when she received the messengers and sent *them* out another way?' (2:25). Placing the two characters side by side in this way brings some theological truths into focus. Abraham was renowned for his lifelong faith whereas Rahab's notoriety, by contrast, reveals an act of faith set against the backdrop of a life of sin. In this we are being taught that no matter how meagre, faith in God leads to justification before God. Even the weakest faith must bear fruit in works, not to earn salvation but as evidence of that reality. Rahab is mentioned to demonstrate that infamous people without distinguished pedigree are as acceptable to God as those of notable lineage. As Scripture tells us: 'God shows personal favouritism to no man' (Gal.2:6).

Rahab obviously believed that God was with Israel. Furthermore, that faith was demonstrated in the way she played a part and risked her life to hide the spies sent by

Joshua. She helped them to escape by sending them on a route that was more likely to assist them in evading capture. In this we see the transforming power of faith demonstrated in new attitudes and actions. God honoured that faith as he always does. It is also evident from her actions that she preferred the glory of God and the good of His people to the preservation of her own country. Some may be inclined to think of her as a traitor who committed a treasonous act against her own people by collaborating with the enemy. Certainly, she betrayed her country, but in doing this she showed a new allegiance. When we come to consider Jonah's allegiances I trust we will come to understand that his sense of patriotism engendered a pride and prejudice that undermined his loyalty to God and the commission entrusted to him.

In considering Rahab we have made the point that God had gracious dealings with people outside Israel. We could equally well convey the same message by considering Ruth, a Moabite woman, who became the great grandmother of King David. Ruth's husband, Boaz, was the son of Rahab. We saw above that Rahab is listed in the genealogy of Jesus but so too is Ruth, in the same verse cited earlier (Mt.1:5).

Ultimately God's plan is that people of every tribe and nation would become beneficiaries of His great grace. God is merciful to the undeserving.

A Peculiar Person

Jonah is unique in that it does not present us with any great detail about the content of the prophetic oration itself. Rather it is about the man commissioned to deliver the message. In this we see that the heart of Jonah contrasts with the heart of God. Jonah knew his God in the sense that he knew something of God's merciful nature. He says: 'I know that You *are* a gracious and merciful God, slow to anger and abundant in lovingkindness, One who relents from doing harm' (4:2). He behaved as if he was unaware of the all-powerful and ever-present nature of God. This is evident in his attempt to flee the presence of God and remove himself from the authority of God. How can we explain such a deficiency in the knowledge of one of God's prophets? Jonah was typical of God's people at this time in that he tended to think that God was active only with His covenant people within the borders of Israel. In fleeing Israel, therefore, he thought, not so much that he was fleeing the presence of God, but leaving the place where there were constant reminders of God's activity and presence. He was in reality fleeing a call to the service of God. Clearly Jonah believed that God ruled as sovereign over the world. He says, "I *am* a Hebrew; and I fear the LORD, the God of heaven, who made the sea and the dry *land*" (1:9). So he knew that by leaving the shores of Israel he could not leave God behind. The text says that, 'Jonah arose to flee...from the presence of the LORD (1:3); and he told the sailors that he was running away from God (1:10). This does not mean that he was trying to hide from the omnipresent God; rather that he was attempting to withdraw from service to God. He hoped that by leaving the land of Canaan, he would leave behind the office and responsibilities of prophet.

We too are aware that we cannot flee from God's presence. We too, know the teaching of Scripture:

> Where can I go from Your Spirit? Or where can I flee from Your presence? If I ascend into heaven, You *are* there; If I make my bed in hell, behold, You *are there. If* I take the wings of the morning, *and* dwell in the uttermost parts of the sea, even there Your hand shall lead me, and Your right hand shall hold me (Ps.139:7-10).

Our disobedience is often in the form of Jonah's. We want to run away, not from the presence of God; we want to withdraw from His service. Disobedience is a matter of the heart; it is not a question of geography. It may be that the act of disobedience will be wrapped in 'seeming providences'. Our backslidings may seem a blessing. Jonah found a ship that was going his way. Matthew Henry says, 'Providence seemed to favour his design, and gave him an opportunity to escape: we may be out of the way of duty, and yet may meet with a favourable gale. The ready way is not always the right way.' If we are not willingly obeying the commands of God, we are effectively fleeing from His presence. We are seeking to restrict God's authority in our lives and exempting ourselves from His control. Jonah fled because of his views of God. He rebelled because of what he knew about God's compassion[5].

Jonah was given a commission to preach against the people; calling for repentance and issuing a message of judgement, "Yet forty days, and Nineveh shall be overthrown!" (3:4) He knew that although he preached judgement God desired to exercise grace and mercy. He knew the heart of God was a forgiving heart that responded to true repentance. So he fled because he was displeased with the possibility that God would show mercy to the heathen world. He is afraid that the preaching of judgement would bring repentance and thus avert from Nineveh the destruction with which it is threatened. Here is another aspect of God's Gospel. Judgement is real for the unrepentant but God offers forgiveness. Jonah knew his God. God's subsequent dealings with him involved a repeated call to carry out the service from which he had turned away.

In Jonah's defence we should say that the commission he was given was without precedent. He was asked to leave the environs of his homeland and go right to the capital city of a hostile people proclaim that their wickedness offended God. This was a difficult and potentially dangerous task. Israel had become a smug, insular, inward looking, self-centred nation. But this begs the question: are the people of God today equally smug, insular, inward looking and self-obsessed?

---

[5] See Jonah 4:2, already cited in the introduction.

Tone

God's commission to Jonah must be understood as a command. The tone is imperative and the mission is important, urgent and obligatory. God did not tell Jonah to go to Nineveh and try to establish friendships so that if an opportunity presented itself then he could tell the Ninevites to think about the possibility that God is not pleased with them. There is an unmistakably authoritative note in both the message and the manner in which it is communicated to Jonah. The Lord said: "Arise, go to Nineveh, that great city, and cry out against it; for their wickedness has come up before Me" (1:2).

The same must be said of the great commission entrusted to those who would follow Christ. Jesus said, "All authority has been given to Me in heaven and on earth. Go therefore and make disciples of all the nations..." (Mt.28:18-19). We must understand the authoritative nature of this commission. It is not merely that God *desires* that we do it; rather he *demands* that we do it.

God did not say to Jonah, "perhaps you might consider going to Nineveh and waiting for opportunities and accepting them, at your discretion." This needs to be stated in an age that is resentful of authority and infatuated with dialogue. There is nothing wrong with friendship evangelism. There is nothing wrong with dialogue per se. We ought to use every means to win people for Christ but those who say that our presence[6] is preferable to proclamation are ignorant of the teaching of Scripture. Those who are interested in church growth strategies need

---

[6] By presence here I am referring to the view that proclaimation is an outmoded means of communicating the gospel and that drawing alongside people (friendship evangelism) is more likely to produce results. Both should go hand in hand. Even in the story of the Philippian jailer (where he takes the initiative in asking, "what must I do to be saved") it is the preaching of Paul and Silas that that led to be in the presence of this man, which in turn led to his conversion.

to realise that the best manuals on this issue are the Gospels, the book of Acts and *Jonah* where preaching is primarily God's means of reaching the lost. We see the importance of presence in the salvation of the Philippian jailer's salvation and by all means let us practice it, but not to the exclusion of proclamation.

Jonah was clearly instructed to enter an antagonistic, pagan culture and condemn it as wicked and call for repentance. As already observed there is a regal and righteous note in the tone of the message. This had the effect of causing the city to humble itself before God and avoid impending doom. Dear Christian, we need to realise that the world despises the gospel. The world can be unsympathetic and unreceptive to the Word of God. The world can be unwelcoming and unpleasant to the messengers of God. We can easily be intimidated by the tough assignment given to us but God has commanded us, God has commissioned us and whether the outcome is favourable or unfavourable in terms of conversions it is our faithfulness in doing His bidding that is what He requires.

The Disposition of our Hearts

By studying this book we can gain valuable insights about the results of disobedience. The lessons illustrated in the life of Jonah show that pride and prejudice led to several negative emotions such as anger and depression. Perhaps a better understanding of this book will cause us to ask, what is the disposition of our hearts? Perhaps we will come to see some negative emotions in our lives resulting from pride and prejudice? Jonah desired to see judgement but God desired to see repentance. How about us today? Do we want God to judge this wicked world or are we mouthpieces of mercy? We must prayerfully consider our own lives and examine our attitudes and actions in the light of Scripture. Are there areas in which we have allowed pride and prejudice to creep in unchecked?

There is no doubt that the task Jonah was given was not a pleasant one. It is fascinating to notice how he responded to the revealed will of God. It is an unexpected response that strikes us as incongruous with the prophetic office. But are we any better in our response to the clear commission entrusted to us as disciples of Christ? God prepared a plan for Jonah and he ran away. In one sense this was a specific commission given to a particular individual in a certain time and place and as such it is Jonah's problem and not ours. However, we could say the same about the great commission entrusted to the disciples of Christ. That too was given to other people at a certain time and specific location. Nevertheless, just as Christ's commission is relevant today Jonah's commission also has a timeless dimension. In order to appreciate this we need to have a clear understanding of the nature of prophecy.

The Nature of Prophecy

It is not right to make a direct connection between the prophet and the preacher. Scripture says: 'God, who at various times and in various ways spoke in time past to the fathers by the prophets, has in these last days spoken to us by *His* Son...' (Heb.1:1-2). However, there is a sense in which all preaching is prophetic. When the preaching of the Scripture is a faithful exposition of the text of God's Word it is a *forth-telling* of the mind of God as revealed in that Word and that is often what the prophets were engaged in doing. This is not the same as a *foretelling* of future events, which was a unique prophetic function under the direction of God. But even in this regard the preacher may say with certainty, for example, that the unrepentant sinner is condemned to spend eternity in hell or that the Lord will return. The Lord has revealed to us, through His Word, something of the future. In this the preacher is not *predicting* the future, rather he is *proclaiming* it. There are parallels in the role of prophet and preacher but that is not to say they are the same. In the preacher's experience there are times when messages have prepared the hearts of God's people for events that were about to take place in their lives. It is not that the preacher has some kind of foreknowledge that those events would take place but God condescended to minister to others in this way through the preaching of His own precious Word.

The prophets of old were the direct mouthpieces of God and they spoke on His behalf. They predicted events, which had not yet happened and in this sense their preaching was a *foretelling* of the future. But their preaching was also an exposition of the law and in this sense it was a *forth telling* of God's mind. It is in this sense that all preaching has a prophetic dimension, or at least it ought to have. Preaching helps people make sense of their experience and it also helps them to make biblically informed choices. It gives a heavenly perspective on earthly and eternal issues. As already mentioned; often Spirit-anointed preaching will prepare people for future events that the preacher could not have known would happen. It is not that they have extra-biblical knowledge. Rather through expository preaching a clearer understanding of God's heart, His nature and work emerges. And frequently this is a Word in season.

A Global Mission

God's plan is a world plan and Christians must not restrict it. We may have limited vision but God does not. The book of *Jonah* challenges us not to be blinkered in our vision for mission or narrow in our prayers or plans for the dissemination of the gospel. Jonah sins and there are consequences arising out of his disobedience. This is one of the important lessons to be learned from *Jonah*: when we go contrary to what God says we get into trouble. It does not matter how trivial our disobedience may seem to us, God takes any departure from His clearly expressed will very seriously indeed. But we must not overlook the fact that Jonah's departure from God's desire centres round the very issue of the extension of God's mercy to undeserving people. God will not allow His redemptive plans to be thwarted by the frailty of His servants.

A Picture of Salvation

In chapter 2 we read of how God prepared a fish to swallow Jonah. The prophet cries out to God from that dreadful place. He realises that he cannot save himself and in this too the message of the gospel is affirmed: salvation is totally a work of God. In fact Jonah's salvation is truly amazing. Even more amazing is our salvation; that God became man and died for us.

Imagine, being in the belly of this great fish. It must have been smelly, noisy, confined and disgusting. Jonah was learning that salvation is a messy business. Our salvation too was a messy business. Anyone who has seen the film, *The Passion of Christ*[7], will realise just how vile and disgusting the scourging of Jesus was. Jonah cried out from the depth of despair and God delivered him.

In chapter 3 we see that God re-commissioned Jonah. In this we see that God does not always choose the 'best' people, nor does He give up on those who let Him down. The book ends with a pertinent question, 'should I not pity Nineveh, that great city...?' (4:11) God's concern is not in doubt but Jonah's lack of concern is called into question. God's concern for the wicked inhabitants of vast cities has not diminished over time. The question we need to ask is; do we share that concern?

Jonah not only presents the pride and prejudice of one of God's most peculiar prophets, but it also portrays the

---

[7]Some might say that Mel Gibson's film was gratuitously violent but in truth it portrays the reality of scourging (as corroborated by historical documents of the time) in a less sanitised way than other films which contain scenes of the passion of Christ.

magisterial and merciful heart of God. Thus a theology of mission is established, not by various Scriptural proof texts alone, but rather in the compassionate character of the Almighty. Both the man and the message will be considered in context. However, we will not confine our comments to the 'then and there' of the biblical text but we will endeavour to bring out the contemporary application for the 'here and now'. Hopefully this will challenge the individual Christian and the church to abandon their inward-looking attitudes and to prioritise mission. I hope that this work will provide a much needed stimulus for evangelism as it reminds us that the church is commissioned in the unfinished task of bringing the gospel to all nations.

1.

Major and Minor Message

Nineveh was the capital city of Assyria at the time of Jonah's ministry. It was a great city in several ways (size, structure, architecture, population and influence). In Jonah's generation Nineveh continued to be one of the most powerful and influential cities of the Assyrian Empire. The Assyrian king had a residence in Nineveh and it was from this city that merchants traded throughout the empire and the city became prosperous. It was one of the most important and prominent cities in the near eastern world of its era.

We are told that, 'Nineveh was an exceedingly great city, a three-day journey *in extent*' (3:3). Many have speculated as to what precisely that means. Perhaps it implies that to visit the entire city would require a three day stay. But maybe the phrase refers to the total area. A reference in Genesis might indicate that Nineveh was part of a greater conurbation of four cities: Nineveh, Rehoboth, Calah and Resen (10:10-12), which may jointly have been referred to as, 'exceedingly great city' that included Nineveh. So it is possible that there was a metropolis of four cities. We need not be certain on this matter. The important issue is that Nineveh was a place of considerable size. Professional authorities in their fields of expertise (archaeologists and historians) think the perimeter was probably about 60 miles. It occupied an area of 350 square miles. The city walls were 100 feet high and were so wide that three chariots could drive abreast along the top of them. Built into this wall were 1,500 towers each of them 200 feet high. It had 15 gates which were guarded by colossal lions and bulls. This was an enormous place. It was 'great' not only in population, significance and size but also in splendour. By any criterion Nineveh was an imposing city which was great in significance, size, structure, population, splendour and influence. However it was also a place of great sin.

We cannot be certain what the exact population of Nineveh was. However we do read that it was a place with 120,000 people who did not know their left hand from their right hand[1]. It is not clear what exactly this means, but we might reasonably say that this is the number of very young children in Nineveh who have not yet reached an age where they know the difference between left and right. We might suppose from this that the population of Nineveh was anything from 750,000 to 2,000,000 people. This would indeed make it a great city in terms of population. But more importantly Nineveh was a great city in terms of its strategic influence. However, we are not primarily concerned with the greatness of the city but with the gravity of the message.

Great Commission

God commands Jonah to 'arise and go'. In some ways Jonah might represent the sleeping church in this crucial hour and Nineveh could be seen to stand for a lost world teetering on the brink of doom and destruction. Jonah refuses to accept the commission entrusted to him by God and on his sea voyage we find him asleep in the middle of a great storm. Are we any different? Are we avoiding our obligations with regard to the commission entrusted to us by the Lord? Are we sleeping while all around there is turmoil? *Jonah* has a contemporary message that should challenge our smugness. We too have been commissioned to bring a message from God to cities where judgement is impending.

---

[1] This might refer to their moral ignorance.

The message given to Jonah and the message given to us, both have an overture of love and mercy. In both there is a call to repentance which will result in God extending forgiveness to those who are truly contrite. This first chapter makes a sad reading because it records the disobedience of God's servant.

> But Jonah arose to flee to Tarshish from the presence of the LORD. He went down to Joppa, and found a ship going to Tarshish; so he paid the fare, and went down into it, to go with them to Tarshish from the presence of the Lord (1:3).

Nineveh was in the East and Tarshish was in the West! He went in the opposite direction. There was no doubt about the revealed will of God, so why did he disobey? We have already addressed the question as to how could a man in his position think it was possible to 'flee the presence of the Lord' Jonah was, after all, a prophet, steeped in the knowledge of the Word of God. He wasn't ignorant of God's omnipresence? I suppose it could be said that just like us he was aware of the truth, but ignored it. We profess faith in the omnipresence, omnipotence and sovereignty of God and at times we behave as if we were completely unaware of these truths. We fail to act in light of the fact that God is everywhere; we fail to act in light of the fact that God is all-powerful and in control. Ultimately the book of *Jonah* graphically illustrates the reality that it is impossible to flee the presence of the Lord. This is potentially *comforting* to the obedient and equally it is potentially *confronting* to the disobedient.

In the Introduction we began to explore what is meant by 'the presence of God' in this context? We asserted that Israel is that place where God made a peculiar manifestation of himself. We discovered that was why Jonah fled to Tarshish. It is worth developing this point a little further. If he was determined not to go to Nineveh he could have stayed in Israel but he fled towards Tarshish, because he wanted to get out of Israel. Israel was the place where the Word of the Lord was heard. The Temple was in that place as a constant reminder to the people of true worship. It was within the borders of Israel that the Law of God was laid up in the Arc of the Covenant. It was there that God established a prophetic ministry. So Jonah wants to flee that place where there are too many vivid reminders that Jehovah is their God and they are to be His loyal subjects. When a child of God wants to choose his own direction and refuses to submit to the Word of the Lord he will avoid people and places that challenge his attitudes and actions. When we want to avoid accountability we will absent ourselves from anything and anybody that will challenge us or confront us with the error of our ways.

The Condition of Jonah's Heart

Although the instruction, "Arise, go to Nineveh" (1:2), is clear, God's representative is rebellious and disobedient. It is amazing that a man who held such an office was more uncooperative to God's stated will than the Ninevites. This was a point of clear departure from God's will.

In our spiritual journey through life we too can know such points of departure. Many of us think that a change of circumstances or a change of location will help us get away from the pressure of God's hand upon our lives or stifle His voice.

Why did Jonah disobey? Some commentators say he feared the credibility of God was at stake or he feared a loss of his own reputation as a prophet. The idea that people might have cause to say, "this man prophesied judgement on Nineveh but it did not happen", may have influenced him but it is not an entirely satisfactory explanation for his rebellious behaviour. This idea does not hold up when scrutinised because Jonah was commissioned to call for repentance in Nineveh. It would always have been clear that genuine contrition would avert the threatened destruction. Every parent understands the principle. A father may threaten punishment on his children if certain behaviour continues but when the child immediately stops the offending behaviour and apologises then the threat of punishment has had the desired effect. There is no need to implement the sanction.

The fact that Jonah refused to obey wasn't anything to do with the journey itself. It was not that the trip to Nineveh would have been too arduous and was, therefore, too daunting for Jonah. The voyage to Tarshish was, in fact, far more hazardous. It has already been noted that the Ninevites were a violent people who tortured and killed their enemies. But it was not fear that deterred Jonah from fulfilling his mission. It was certainly not because of cowardice as is sometimes thought and taught. This is evident in his attitude during the storm at sea when he asked the crew of the ship to throw him overboard. Death would be the expected outcome of such action. Obviously, therefore, Jonah was not afraid to die. So, if Jonah was neither bothered by the thought of an arduous journey nor afraid to die why then did he try to avoid doing what God told him to do? The answer to this question is quite shocking. Jonah fled because he understood the character of God. He knew the Lord to be gracious. We need be in no doubt about this matter because we read:

> So he prayed to the LORD, and said, "Ah, LORD, was not this what I said when I was still in my country? Therefore I fled previously to Tarshish; for I know that You are a gracious and merciful God, slow to anger and abundant in lovingkindness, One who relents from doing harm" (4:2).

This statement is reminiscent of Exodus 34 where God discloses to Moses that He is a God of mercy, patience and love, in name and nature.

Jonah had an intense patriotism which clouded his judgement. His unwillingness to go to Nineveh was rooted in the prejudiced but prevalent idea that Gentile nations were beyond the scope of God's merciful activity. To put it bluntly, the thought that these pagan Ninevites would be the object of God's mercy sickened him. In this regard Jonah is a specimen Israelite inasmuch as he mirrors the spirit of the entire nation. They were elitist and exclusive. They had ceased to regard themselves as favoured recipients of grace and were devoid of any understanding that they should be a light to the Gentiles. They saw themselves as the sole beneficiaries of God's affections and as worthy objects of His favour and love. They had begun to think of themselves as God's pet people and they expected that He would dote on them and lavish His affection and gifts on them to the exclusion of the rest of the world. But God never intended it to be so.

Are there some Christians today who, although shocked and amazed that Israel could have so greatly misunderstood God's purposes, are equally misguided? God does not confine His activity to the church. God is as active among heathen, harlots and heretics today, as he has always been in every generation. There are those who would like us to believe that God cannot work among such people or circumstances or within certain systems, be they political, religious cultural or otherwise. This is not so.

Jonah needed a vision of the largeness of the heart of God and so do we, because we too are guilty of a lack of love and a love of ease! The church can be inward looking but there is an important and abiding principle which we need to bear in mind; whenever we turn our eyes inward, towards ourselves, our problems, our accomplishments or wounded egos, we turn our eyes away from God and away from others. As we examine the condition of Jonah's heart let us ask ourselves; what is the condition of our own hearts?

The Chastening of Jonah

Scripture clearly teaches that the Lord chastens His children:

"My son, do not despise the chastening of the LORD, nor be discouraged when you are rebuked by Him; for whom the LORD loves He chastens, and scourges every son whom He receives." If you endure chastening, God deals with you as with sons; for what son is there whom a father does not chasten? But if you are without chastening, of which all have become partakers, then you are illegitimate and not sons. Furthermore, we have had human fathers who corrected *us,* and we paid *them* respect. Shall we not much more readily be in subjection to the Father of spirits and live? For they indeed for a few days chastened *us* as seemed *best* to them, but He for *our* profit, that *we* may be partakers of His holiness. Now no chastening seems to be joyful for the present, but painful; nevertheless, afterward it yields the peaceable fruit of righteousness to those who have been trained by it (Heb.12:4-11).

In the storm we see that God pursues His people and that God's purposes are being fulfilled in our trials. Many of God's children have tried to flee the clear call of God. There may be some strategic area of your life where you are defying or ignoring the will of the Lord. This can result in a raging storm in your life that affects not only yourself but everyone around you.

In the story of this man we see weakness in the best of men. Here is a man who had the privilege of direct communication with God. It was his culture that distorted his perspective. We might well ask; what traditions and customs in our blood and backgrounds can blind us to the purposes of God for this world? The sad reality is that there is a tragic potential for disobedience in the heart of every believer, whatever his role in the kingdom.

Major and Minor plot

The theme of the book of *Jonah* has been identified as a revelation of the largeness of the heart of God. However there is also a major and a minor plot in the book of *Jonah.*

In other words, there is an interrelationship of events in this biblical book. If the major plot deals with the restoration of a disobedient prophet then the minor plot deals with the spiritual enlightenment of the pagan sailors. This minor plot is woven into the fabric of the story and serves to illustrate the thematic purpose of the book by demonstrating that God is not a limited, local, tribal deity. Both aspects of the narrative work in harmony towards the fulfilment of God's purposes. God is concerned to bring His disobedient child back into communion with Himself and equally concerned that His message should get to Nineveh.

The sub plot begins in chapter 1 where we read: 'Then the mariners were afraid; and every man cried out to his god…' (1:5). Initially, there is a manifestation of their crude paganism but eventually these men come to some knowledge of God. Belief in the immortality and accountability of the soul is fundamental to all religions. A. W. Tozer said, 'Religion, so far as it is genuine, is in essence the response of created personalities to the creating personality of God.' The sailors were genuinely afraid of losing their lives and while Jonah was in a deep sleep below in the deck, they were busy tossing the cargo into the sea in order to save the vessel from sinking. However, when Jonah is aroused and he confesses that he is an Israelite and that he worships the God who made the sea, they are terrified. The phrase 'exceedingly afraid' in verse 10 refers, not merely to physical fear, but to a deep religious awe. Verse 14 says they cried out to 'the Lord', not *a god*, not *the gods* but that they called upon Jehovah, the covenant God of Israel. Then verse 16 speaks of their *sacrifice* and *vows* to Jehovah. In this act they are binding themselves to lives of covenant obligation. Whether they kept these promises or reneged on them is another matter. What does matter is that here are all the essential ingredients of true heart religion, which began with a reverential awe of the living God.

This storm, sent and sustained by God, is the physical element of God's creation, and these heathen sailors are the moral element of His creation working in harmony towards Gods purpose; to bring Jonah to his senses. These were experienced sailors who were not afraid of a few waves. They were well used to sailing in squalls and swells. But on this occasion they hear the very structure of the ship creaking and realise that the vessel is in imminent danger of sinking.

They are certain that there is a connection between the heaving tempest and somebody on board. We could say they were merely superstitious but in truth were they not correct? What we learn about these men from this incident is that they are inherently religious. Matthew Henry said, 'The root of religion is the fear of God reigning in the heart, a reverence of his majesty, a deference to his authority and a dread of his wrath.' They want to know who is guilty of provoking God. They cried out to *the Lord*. This shows that they acknowledge that there is a supreme being who stands above their lesser 'gods'. Furthermore, they acknowledge the relationship between the pleasure and displeasure of this God and the physical world. They recognise that this God controls the elements of the world. They exhort Jonah: "Arise, call on your god!" Thus they accept that this God is accessible through prayer. So here you have the essential ingredients of a religious constitution. At a minimum we can allow that there is evidence of a fundamental theism, albeit in the midst of superstition and error. Yet God is at work in their activity as much as He is in the activity of the storm.

These men, at a time of crisis, are drawn to God and in their distress they call out to God for salvation.[2] In many Western societies today the appearance of prevailing secularism may be deceptive because some societies still retain a sense of the reality of God. There is in such societies

---

[2] Their primary concern is to be rescued from this storm and as such they are seeking a temporal salvation.

a residual theism and despite religious superstition and error this fundamental belief in God can be an opening for the entrance of the gospel. In a metaphorical sense we might say there are times of crises when storms are raging and people become afraid that the creaking timbers of their ship (i.e. the institutions in which they trust) will not survive in such tempestuous waters. On such occasions people will search for answers. Jonah slept, while the storm raged. In such tumultuous times Christians should not be found slumbering.

The frightening implication of the storm in Jonah is that it is a result of Jonah's disobedient refusal to fulfil the charge entrusted to him. People in our society are being tossed about like corks in violent storms of confusion because we too are neglecting to fulfil the commission assigned to us. We must be awake and alert and bear testimony to our God. One might say it is difficult to comprehend how Jonah could sleep in circumstances like this, but perhaps the church today is slumbering at a time of crisis in the world when the very destruction of the planet is threatened by man's greed and reckless disregard for the stewardship of ecology.

The Process of Restoration Begins

There comes a point in the story where the process of restoration begins and it must be acknowledged that that process has a divine initiative. We have considered the diversity of means employed by God (such as the elements of the physical creation and elements of the moral creation) to bring Jonah back on track. There is the arousal of the prophet from his state of slumber (1:6). He is indicted for his sin of disobedience (1:7-8). He makes an honest confession (1:9-10). He submitted to the just deserts of that sin as far as the temporal punishment is concerned (1:11-15). Then we read his prayer for deliverance (2:1-9). It is extraordinary that Jonah did not pray before the sailors threw him overboard. Even at that point, faced with the prospect of death, he continued in his obstinacy. But God created the circumstances which brought Jonah to a place of prayer. What must God bring into our lives in order to bring us to a place of receptivity to His will?

He prayed in a peculiar place. Not a place one would choose! However, it was where he was at the time and that is always the place to pray. God heard and answered him. God has the power to hear and answer sincere prayer from the most peculiar locations. Irrespective of the details of this prayer it is clear from the act of prayer itself that Jonah knew instinctively that it was not possible to flee the presence of the Almighty.

The Where, Why and When of Prayer

Jonah is brought back to the place in his experience where his disobedience began and reflection on the futility of his actions stimulates the desire to obey. This same process by which Jonah was restored to obedience is the process by which every sinning, disobedient child of God is brought back into communion with God and into fellowship. The first step is arousal from slumber; that state of spiritual lethargy. Are there areas in our lives where the Word of God has come to us but we are going in a different direction? Jonah prayed in a time of affliction and distress, but we don't have to wait until we are in trouble to pray. He prayed when his life was ebbing away. We should not allow our circumstances to become so critical before approaching God. Jonah was now at the end of himself. There would be no more running away.

Jonah is delivered and God's call is renewed and in this we see that it is never too late to be used by God. There are numerous biblical examples of God's grace bestowed on those who had spectacularly failed Him; men like the apostle Peter and the Old Testament king, David. God can reach us wherever we are today! However, we may be indicted by God for our prayerlessness because we are in a sense, asleep while others are crying out to their gods. Jonah confesses God as his creator and sees his place in the plan of things as a privileged Hebrew and prophet. Jonah must have thought it was all over for him; that he was washed up! Perhaps he thought deliverance was the best that could happen and he probably doubted that God would ever use him again. Nevertheless, the second call came in spite of the fact that Jonah would fail again!

He was displeased with Nineveh's repentance and disappointed with his own success. This is a strange preacher who regrets that God used him; an evangelist who is pouting over a whole city of penitents! What hard hearts we have and still God loves us and uses us. The gracious message of *Jonah* is that whatever our past, God will meet us today, even if we are weak and even if we will fail again tomorrow! The story moves forward with the renewed commission of the wayward prophet (3:1-2); the response of the prophet (3:3-4) and the repentance of the Ninevites (3:5-9).

Renewed Commission

The God of Israel speaks once again in regal majesty and in sovereign authority: 'Now the word of the Lord came to Jonah the second time, saying, "Arise, go to Nineveh, that great city, and preach to it the message that I tell you"(3:2). Once again this is a sovereign act of God. He does not consult Jonah or negotiate with His subject. God simply instructs Jonah to, "Arise, go to Nineveh…and preach…" There is no cajoling or pleading. Rather, he comes in the full exercise of His rights and prerogatives as the God-King of Israel and commands.

In conservative evangelical churches on Sundays there is no opportunity for discussion or dialogue. Some people are critical of this didactic style of teaching because it is foreign to their whole sphere of reference. We live in an age where there is great resentment against anybody who would have the nerve to proclaim *the truth*. People today like to flatter themselves with the idea that they can discover spiritual truth for themselves. But the idea that almighty God should come and command is anathema to them.

I believe in prophetic preaching (explained earlier), not as a foretelling of future events but a forth-telling of the mind of God from Scripture. I believe in preaching that has a note of sovereignty in the exposition of His Word and no matter what the latest trends in ecclesiology it must always be central to church life. We live in an age where there is resentment against anybody who has the nerve to tell people what to do and how to live their lives. Nevertheless Christians are a people who claim that the Word of God has authority in their lives. We must, therefore yield to its rule.

This is a gracious re-commissioning. Think of the man to whom this Word came; the first time he fled. The man whose record is before us in the first commission took the bit in his teeth determined not go to Nineveh but to go to in the opposite direction to Tarshish. He had to be dealt with in a strange way to be brought to obedience. God could have said: "You blew it and your disobedience once, to so clear a commission, shows that you are unfit for the solemn responsibilities of being my prophet." That would have been reasonable. God could have said: "I will find another messenger because you failed and therefore forfeited your usefulness as a mouthpiece of God." But here is the God of grace restoring and re-commissioning His servant; giving him the opportunity to go back and make amends.

The renewed commission is clear and unambiguous. There is much talk today about finding the will of God for one's life. But there is so much of the will of God that is explicitly stated for all believers that there is hardly a need for such an emphasis. Of course the believer should seek God's will for his life but there is much he need not search out because there is much that is clearly revealed. The question is; are we adhering to the expressed will of God?

When did Jesus rescind that great commission?

> "All authority has been given to Me in heaven and on earth. Go therefore and make disciples of all the nations, baptizing them in the name of the Father and of the Son and of the Holy Spirit, teaching them to observe all things that I have commanded you; and lo, I am with you always, *even* to the end of the age" (Mt.28:18-20).

Has it been revoked? And how have so many come to consider themselves exempt from it? Are their areas of our lives where the Word of God has come to you with clarity and you are ignoring it?

Are you like Jonah? Have you been aroused from your state of inertia? Is your conscience tormented? Is your spirit broken? Have you come to the point where you desire to be reconciled with God? Do you have a dark cloud above your head? Are you wondering if you can ever go back to the point of your disobedience and begin again? Go back and plead with Him that it might please Him to magnify His grace in restoring you!

2.

Right Responses

The Response of the Prophet

> So Jonah arose and went to Nineveh, according to the word of
> the LORD. Now Nineveh was an exceedingly great city, a
> three-day journey *in extent*. And Jonah began to enter the city
> on the first day's walk. Then he cried out and said, "Yet forty
> days, and Nineveh shall be overthrown!" (3:3-4)

It is reasonable to assume that these words are the theme of his message and do not constitute the entire content. They are a summary of the main thrust of his preaching. In the same way as the sermons in Acts and the activity of Jesus are selected highlights.[3] The words, "Yet forty days and Nineveh shall be overthrown!" were probably expounded and explained in preaching that was intelligible and meaningful. It may be that he walked through the streets of Nineveh proclaiming only these words over and over again, but I am inclined to think otherwise. In reality we simply do not know. In any case his message states the intention of God to overthrow this great but wicked city and this is clearly understood by those who heard him. Perhaps Jonah even gave his testimony. Certainly his prayer reads like it is also a message which could be delivered as a personal declaration of God's gracious dealings with him.

What is important to consider here is the fact that God issued an explicit command to His servant and this

---

[3] See Jn.21:25

time the response was unequivocal obedience. There is no prevarication, no beating about the bush, no fudging the issue or quibbling about the matter. Jonah does not seek any further clarification; there is no more delaying.

This is the essence of returning from spiritual backsliding; the acid test. Does the Word of God now hold sway in your life in areas where His Word was previously ignored, defied and disobeyed? Repentance is not just an emotional experience. The measure of the genuineness of spiritual restoration is not merely to be found in the degree of emotional upheaval experienced when God shook you as he shook Jonah. The true measure of genuine restoration is not merely professing renewed communion with God. The litmus test is found right here: does the Word of God, which was once disobeyed, now capture you in the precise areas where your disobedience was manifested? Jesus said: "If you love me you will keep my commandments."

A person may be aroused from spiritual sleep, feel the terrors of a tormented conscience, be desperately sorry and yet fail to fulfil the commission entrusted to him. Going to God whimpering and whining with such fervency that you have the salve of some kind of emotional release applied to your conscience is one thing, but obedience is another! Have you forsaken your sins? Are you still running from the Word of the Lord that impinges on your life as a husband, father, wife, mother, son or daughter? Scripture says, 'godly sorrow produces repentance...' (2 Cor.7:10).

The Repentance of Nineveh

> So the people of Nineveh believed God, proclaimed a fast, and put on sackcloth, from the greatest to the least of them. Then word came to the king of Nineveh; and he arose from his throne and laid aside his robe, covered *himself* with sackcloth and sat in ashes. And he caused *it* to be proclaimed and published throughout Nineveh by the decree of the king and his nobles, saying, Let neither man nor beast, herd nor flock, taste anything; do not let them eat, or drink water. But let man and beast be covered with sackcloth, and cry mightily to God; yes,

> let every one turn from his evil way and from the violence that
> is in his hands. Who can tell *if* God will turn and relent, and
> turn away from His fierce anger, so that we may not perish?
> (3:5-9).

Verse 5 encapsulates their response: 'the people of Nineveh believed God, proclaimed a fast, and put on sackcloth, from the greatest to the least of them.' The remainder of the passage cited above gives a detailed account of the repentance itself.

Their repentance had a particular focus on violence (3:8) which Jonah probably denounced. The king's decree is quite detailed about the manner in which his subjects should abase themselves before God. It is possible or probable that Jonah gave instruction in this matter. True repentance would involve more than mere observance of these external things. True repentance is a matter of the heart and must be sincerely meant for the possibility of any efficacious outcome. Repentance is also an individual matter. There was, obviously, heartfelt and widespread[4] repentance amongst the Ninevites. Jonah's earlier prayer states: 'those who cling to worthless idols forfeit the grace that could be theirs' (2:8). It seems that none of the Ninevites forfeited the grace of God on this occasion and therefore we must conclude that they forsook their idolatry. Furthermore, the New Testament confirms this: "The men of Nineveh will rise up in the judgment with this generation and condemn it, because they repented at the preaching of Jonah; and indeed, a greater than Jonah *is* here!" (Mt.12:41).

We are told that 'the people of Nineveh believed God' (3:5). Manifestly there was a believing reception to the Word of God and that is the first step in true repentance. There

---

[4] Whether it was unanimous or universal repentance among the populace is not certain. However, they repented in sufficient mass to warrant the aversion of God's wrath. The fact that there is no mention of any individual (s) being destroyed lends credence to the idea that their repentance was universal.

was a thorough dealing with their sin. They did everything necessary to manifest the genuineness of it.

Jesus said, "For as Jonah became a sign to the Ninevites, so also the Son of Man will be to this generation" (Lk.11:30). Jonah probably bore testimony to the details of God's dealings with him and in this sense the man and the message were inextricably linked. Jonah himself became a message, in spite of his wilful disobedience and perhaps even because of it. He was a letter from God saying that God will not be disobeyed and His purposes will not be prevented or perverted. Scarred emotionally, and possibly even physically bearing signs of his ordeal, he was a message that they could read.[5] In many ways this is true of us. Our lives are a message that others can read. People may never come under the sound of preaching, they may not read the *Bible* or Christian literature but they can read the lives of believers and even the mistakes we make and the scars we bear tell a story of Gods power and mercy.

We have this same message for wicked individuals and cities: if you die impenitent, you will be damned. There is a day fixed for your death and the wrath of God hangs over your head unless you repent. The Christian message is this: abandon your wicked ways, cast aside your doubts and fears and come to the cross, because this is the only way to be fit to meet the holy God.

The Ninevites had merely a hopeful plea for mercy, but we can come with a confident prayer for forgiveness: 'If we confess our sins, He is faithful and just to forgive us *our* sins and to cleanse us from all unrighteousness' (1 Jn.1:9). We come not with an optimistic plea (like the Ninevites)

---

[5] Perhaps his skin was affected by the corrosive ingredients of the digestive acid from the stomach of the fish. There are relatively recent documented cases of people who have survived being swallowed alive by whales who emerged after several days with their skin blemished (having a blotchy appearance) as a result of prolonged contact with the creature's digestive enzymes. Thus he, likely, bore the effects of rebellion in his appearance.

but with certainty on the basis of the finished work of Jesus and the promise of His Word.

Jonah's message rings a note of sovereign righteousness and yet it is suffused with grace. God takes a disobedient servant and restores him to the path of obedience. Even though his heart was only half in the message, God imbued it with power and they believed God, repented of their sins and pleaded for mercy. It is true that God accomplishes His work, not because of our involvement but rather in spite of our involvement. Sometimes the messenger of God is more a hindrance than a help. God once spoke to the prophet, Baalam, through the beast of burden who was carrying him: an ass! God didn't need Jonah. It is astonishing that God did not select somebody else to bring the message to Nineveh. Perhaps the reason God selected Jonah is to show us how wrong our attitudes can be. Jonah was on a journey of self-discovery and more than that he was on a journey to the heart of God. Thus it is in the spiritual life where we learn about ourselves through our experiences but more than that may we learn more of God and be increasingly transformed into His likeness. Considering this short biblical book can teach us much about ourselves and God.

What a gospel we preach! In spite of our weaknesses and waywardness His Word is Wonderful and powerful to accomplish His purposes. We must always be conscious of the fact that we too have a great and grave message and that we are commissioned to bring this good news and message of hope to those who repent. As John says, 'For God so loved the world that He gave His only begotten Son, that whoever believes in Him should not perish but have everlasting life' (Jn.3:16). A couple of chapters later the same gospel writer records the words of Jesus: "Most assuredly, I say to you, he who hears My word and believes in Him who sent Me has everlasting life, and shall not come into judgment, but has passed from death into life" (Jn.5:24). This is entirely consistent with the teaching of the Old Testament:

> Seek the LORD while He may be found, Call upon Him while He is near. Let the wicked forsake his way, And the unrighteous man his thoughts; Let him return to the LORD, And He will have mercy on him; And to our God, For He will abundantly pardon' (Isa.55:6-7).

The Response of God to the Ninevites

The reader is presented with a great contrast between the heart of Jonah and the heart of God (3:10-4:11). This contrast is one of the main strands of the book and this section of Scripture highlights the issue. Jonah's heart is narrow, shrivelled and constricted. God's heart is expansive and vast and full to overflowing with mercy and grace. This contrast is set before us in the most vivid way. God bestows blessing but Jonah begrudges this to the Ninevites. Obviously he has forgotten; if he ever understood in the first place, not only that nobody deserves God's blessing but that everybody deserves Gods wrath.

First of all, it is necessary to clarify the fact that God does not change.[6] He is by nature immutable. We should understand that the Ninevites avail of the mercy extended to them rather than thinking that God responded to their repentance. Jonah presents us with this issue: 'Then God saw their works, that they turned from their evil way; and God relented from the disaster that He had said He would bring upon them, and He did not do it' (3:10).

The phrase 'God saw' does not merely refer to knowledge of what happened. It does not mean that God only became aware of it at that point. That is the human perspective, but the divine perspective is quite different. But neither does it refer exclusively to God's omniscience. Certainly God knows all things and knows them before they occur but the phrase 'God saw' means, importantly, that He took it to heart. God is not a mere observer of their

---

[6] See Malachi 3:6 'For I am the LORD, I do not change…'

repentance. He was the author of it. He worked in their hearts! He took the initiative. So here is God beholding the fruit of His own mighty works, with delight! In the Parables of the Lost Coin, The Lost Sheep and The Lost Son (the prodigal) we note that in each case the 'owner' of that which was lost overflows with joy when it is found.[7] Scripture informs us that there is joy in the presence of the angels when one sinner repents.

So what does Scripture mean when it states that God 'relented'? It does not mean that He changed His mind. The book of Jeremiah contains a helpful insight into this issue.

> The instant I speak concerning a nation and concerning a kingdom, to pluck up, to pull down, and to destroy *it*, if that nation against whom I have spoken turns from its evil, I will relent of the disaster that I thought to bring upon it. And the instant I speak concerning a nation and concerning a kingdom, to build and to plant *it*, if it does evil in My sight so that it does not obey My voice, then I will relent concerning the good with which I said I would benefit it (Jer.18:7-10).

Nineveh is a classic example of the teaching of Jeremiah 18. There is a living interaction between God and the Ninevites. Their sin is precipitating judgement but God is saying if this condition changes His response will be different.

This does not in any way invalidate the fixed decrees and sovereign purposes of God. Judgement is contingent upon certain realities. The revealed activity of God is the only valid commentary on the character and purposes of God. Scripture shows His redemptive plans unfolding throughout history. The pulse of chapter 4 of Jonah throbs to the rhythm of God's gracious heart. He takes no sadistic pleasure in judgement. God never brings judgement until the cup of iniquity is so full that to allow it to go unpunished

---

[7] See Luke 15.

would be a contradiction of His moral character. Even then He does it with some measure of reluctance. The sovereign, eternal, omnipotent God of the *Bible* is a living God, not a detached, distant and aloof God of fate.

Much of the production of goods today is automated. There are computerised systems where certain buttons are pushed and it is impersonal, a machine produces the end product. Whatever was decreed by the computer programme will be the outcome. This is how some people understand God. But this is a false picture of God. It is not that somewhere in the distant past God fed everything into the programme and has pushed certain buttons and now sits back and watches it all unfold and makes sure there are no breakdowns or short circuits in the system and if there are He will mend them. The God of the Bible is not detached from the outworking of the details of our lives. This passage in *Jonah* underscores that intimate, sensitive involvement of the living, personal God with His creatures. He desires intimacy with you in the outworking of the details of your life.

The Reaction of Jonah

It is interesting to examine the reaction of Jonah to the merciful dispensation of God. How many preachers have longed to have such a response? He was welcomed as a messenger of God. He should have rejoiced at this dazzling manifestation of the gracious character of God. He should have danced for joy! But he was like the elder brother of the prodigal (Lk.15). He can't stand it when mercy is shown to the undeserving. Are we ever like that? Do we ever resent the way God blesses others? Do we ever want our pound of flesh?

In chapter 2 the problematic prophet had prayed in a manner that was disciplined by the thought patterns of the Scripture (or at least what existed of Scripture at that point in history). He struggles in prayer, to faith and confidence in God, until it reaches its climax in the statement, 'Salvation comes from the Lord'. These are the concluding words of His recorded prayer (2:9). However, by the time we come to read the opening three verses of chapter 4 we see that the petulant, pouting, peevish and prejudiced Jonah is once again on display. He is entirely churlish in this later prayer and has the temerity to remonstrate with God.

> But it displeased Jonah exceedingly, and he became angry. So he prayed to the LORD, and said, "Ah, LORD, was not this what I said when I was still in my country? Therefore I fled previously to Tarshish; for I know that You *are* a gracious and merciful God, slow to anger and abundant in lovingkindness, One who relents from doing harm. Therefore now, O LORD, please take my life from me, for *it is* better for me to die than to live!" (4:1-3).

This is quite a departure from the patterns of Scripture which had shaped his earlier prayer in chapter 2. Prejudice had not only entered his heart but it was now enthroned there!

At this point God rebukes Jonah. God had been merciful to him. He sent the storm and the fish, which may have seemed like punishments but they were actually divine providences to bring Jonah back into the right path of service. The Lord brought the prophet's feet into the way of duty but his heart had not followed. Now God wants to work on his heart. God does not want us to fulfil duties; He wants us to fulfil duties, *joyfully*. It is possible to go to church regularly but reluctantly and this is not what God wants *from* us or *for* us. We can give of our time and money grudgingly and in so doing deprive ourselves of the joy that ought to be part of giving and serving.

God questions Jonah, "*Is it* right for you to be angry?" (4:4) but this does not seem to induce any meaningful self-reflection for Jonah. Nevertheless, God's question is corrective in that it is really a rhetorical statement which can be interpreted to read: "you have no right to be angry." The Word of God is often the first instrument in the restoration of wayward hearts into His will. A question sent from God can bring us to our senses. But in Jonah's case he admits, not that he had *felt* justifiably angry but that he, even now, continues to *feel he has good cause to be* angry. This attitude is a sad reality in the lives of many believers who are unwilling to let go of wrong attitudes towards others and even towards God. We read:

> And the LORD God prepared a plant and made it come up over Jonah, that it might be shade for his head to deliver him from his misery. So Jonah was very grateful for the plant. But as morning dawned the next day God prepared a worm, and it *so* damaged the plant that it withered. And it happened, when the sun arose, that God prepared a vehement east wind; and the sun beat on Jonah's head, so that he grew faint. Then he wished death for himself, and said, "*It is* better for me to die than to live" (6-8).

This plant had a transitory existence in that the vine would ultimately wither and die, but Nineveh was full of immortal souls. God is effectively saying to Jonah, 'How can you think more of the vine than the Ninevites?' But are we any different? Do we spend more time tending our gardens than in evangelism, or prayer for the lost and lonely of this world? Whatever our hobby may be we need to see where it fits in our priorities. Suppose God were to touch the things in your life; the things that provide a kind of shelter from the burning heat of life, and take them away. Something with which your affections have become intertwined: how would you feel? Would you be angry about it?

We all have objects that occupy that space in our affections that should be filled with concern for the lost. This is a powerful word to us as believers. Jonah's heart was carnal and stubborn. Consider the patience and kindness of God.[8] We should plead for hearts that conform more and more to the heart of God. God's message to Jonah is this: "it is not enough that you speak My words, you ought also to feel My feelings." It is a sobering word for the unconverted. What will be your end if you spurn God's grace and face Him impenitent and unconverted? There is an urgent appeal in this book not only to the Ninevites but also to people today. Are we willing to leave the safe precincts of the church and go to a world that is under judgement to bring the message of the gospel? May we have that vision of the largeness and tenderness of the heart of God that impels us to reach out to others!

Summary

The historicity of the story of *Jonah* is accepted and authenticated by Jesus who refers to *Jonah* and treats it as reality. The fact that Jonah is a historical character is important in determining our approach to the text. It is narrative in style and historical in content. Some people have difficulty accepting it as factual because they have a poor understanding of the supernatural power of God.

Jonah is a biographical snapshot of the prophet's commissioning to a specific ministry. It details his disobedience and re-commissioning as well as the consummation of the task to which he was appointed. It is an extremely fitting book to study in the light of world conditions. I trust that a re-examination of this vivid Old Testament picture will enable it to become more meaningful in assisting us in our experience and understanding of God.

Reflections for Today

Jonah enables us to gain valuable insights about the results of disobedience because these insights are illustrated in his

---

[8] The kindness and patience of God is not limitless, as some might suppose, there is a time when He judges and punishes.

life. We learn from observing him that his pride and prejudice and self-centredness ultimately led to several negative emotions such as anger and depression. The lessons of *Jonah* should cause us to consider our own lives. Is there an area in which you have become preoccupied with yourself and your feelings to the exclusion of others? Does pride or prejudice prevent you from reaching people with the gospel? God had given him a task but he ran away. When we disobey God it is sin. It does not matter how trivial it may seem; if we go contrary to His revealed will we get into trouble.

The Task

The task that Jonah was given was not a pleasant one and it is interesting to notice how he responded to the revealed will of God. He was blinkered and limited God to the status quo. Sometimes I wonder if, as believers, we not only *accept* things the way they are but we have come to *expect* them to continue like that. Not only that but it seems that that is how we want things to be! We don't want a great influx of 'undesirables' into our churches and having them bring foreign ideas to the member's meetings and passing motions that change the way we do things. It is cosy the way it is. We are used to each other. We don't want to rock the boat or push it out too far from shore. Numerous foreign converts would drastically change the dynamics of our church and challenge our conservatism. We would have to stop whining about foreigners taking our jobs. We might have to stop saying, 'they' are really only economic migrants and not actually entitled to refugee status. We would be restricted in when and where we could say, 'we don't know their history and backgrounds'.

Perhaps we don't want certain people because their instinct is to dance and clap their hands and shout out comments when we're preaching and we might not be able to control them. The poor and uneducated are an embarrassment.

We are happy with our white, middle-class, Anglo-Saxon, educated and conservative types. No lefties or radicals because we can't handle people who are pro-Palestinian, anti-Israeli and talk about 'state terrorism' in the Middle-East. This makes the home *Bible* study difficult.

We want to handle cultural integration on our terms and our 'welcome' is a conditional form of tokenism. We want our pride and prejudices. Church is the last bastion of 'free speech' where we can pay lip-service to the lost and lament the wickedness of this world. We are proud of our religious heritage. We are proud of religious observance. We are proud of our righteousness and we are going to protect ourselves from any possible contamination which might arise out of 'successful' evangelism.

The gospel is a world message. God's plan is a world plan and our vision should be global in its scale. There is an environmental slogan which seems appropriate for evangelism: 'think globally, act locally.'

3.

Peculiar People

Jonah is a peculiar character. He is pleased with some things and not with others. He is pleased with the vine that gave him shade from the blazing heat. He is displeased that the Ninevites were spared from destruction. Jonah was selective in his appreciation of God's activity. I wonder, if we are ever like that. From whom would we want God to withhold mercy? Are there categories of people whom we deem to be deserving of destruction? Do we ever find ourselves saying, perhaps when we hear of some awful thing in the news: 'I'm glad there is a hell'. Do we consign people to hell in our thoughts?

'Now the word of the LORD came to Jonah the second time' (3:1). Imagine, Jonah staggering up the beach after his ordeal. He must have looked a mess. At last he is on solid ground and he is immediately told to go to Nineveh and proclaim the message the Lord would give to him. He wanted to get away and after all that he had been through he found himself confronted with the same issue he had tried to leave behind. Do we sometimes want to get out from under God's influence? When we are on holidays abroad God is still with us. No matter what the culture or creed of the people in some distant land God is still there. We can never get away from God's presence. Whatever the circumstances in which the children of God find themselves, they may be sure that it is either ordained by God or allowed by God. We are subject to His active or permissive will.

What about Jonah's free will? He clearly decided not to follow the instructions of God but God constrained him. Was he not coerced? What can we say to the charge that God forced him to do something he didn't want to do? Is this evidence that God is a bully and that we had better do as He tells us or suffer dire consequences. Why didn't God ask somebody else? It is clear that Jonah was very determined not to go to Nineveh because it seems he did not pray immediately upon entering the fish. It would appear that he waited three days before calling out to God. This is stubbornness that beggars belief, but it does present us with an important question. Are we free to say "no" to God? If we refuse to obey will he punish us and pursue us until we give in? Is that fair?

First, it must be said that Jonah exercised his freedom of choice. We are not robots programmed to make decisions approved by God. Second, it must be said that a bully is a person who coerces another through fear. Nowhere in the book of *Jonah* is there any indication that Jonah was afraid of God. On the contrary, he spoke to God in a manner which indicates he was not afraid of Him. Third, we must bear in mind the peculiar relationship between Jonah and God. Jonah was, after all, a divinely commissioned prophet. This relationship is important because it is a superior/ subordinate relationship. It might be helpful for us to think of it in terms of a boss giving instructions to his employee. Suppose workers go on strike because of what they perceive to be changes in their work practices. The boss is not bullying his employees if, for example, he takes legal action to prove that his demands are not outside the remit of their contractual obligations. Is the employer not entitled to compel his workers to fulfil certain responsibilities? Fourth, it is likely that nobody else would have accepted such a commission to go to Nineveh. This puts the magnitude of the task and the necessity of getting Jonah to cooperate into perspective. It is really a matter of understanding God's authority in the household of faith and in particular with regard to those who would minister His Word.

Even though Jonah's circumstances would have appeared to indicate otherwise, God's providences were serving His sovereign purpose. Matthew Henry said, 'God's providences often seem to contradict his purposes, even when they are serving them'. Sometimes it is difficult to read God's providences in our lives or the lives of others. We may find it difficult to make sense of the circumstances in which we find ourselves. Martin Luther likened it to a printer who sets the letters backwards and that we will only see the print in the next life. It could also be compared to a great tapestry. God is weaving different coloured threads to create a vast and intricate picture. But often in this life we only see the reverse side of the tapestry where there are a myriad of tangled threads and knots that seem to have no pattern at all.

One suspects there may be many Jonah's in the church today. They have heard the call of God to ministry or mission or some form of service and they are ignoring God. Are you a Jonah whom God is calling to service? Many of us want to pick the role we will play and the places we will go. We reserve the right to say, 'I'm not going there or there', or 'I'm not doing this or that'. But God wants us to fit in with His strategic plans. Have you been stifling the voice of God? Have you been suppressing the knowledge that God desires you to serve Him in some particular way?

Jonah was to learn what George Muller said: 'God not only orders our steps; he orders our stops'. His plans are never thwarted. God not only rules but He also overrules. William Cowper wrote: 'God moves in a mysterious way his wonders to perform; he plants his footsteps in the sea and rides upon the storm.' How true this was in the life of Jonah. God went to great lengths to get Jonah to do His bidding. Jonah is brought to a place of prayer. One might expect the rest of the story to unfold differently from this point. The story of *Jonah* shows that God is very patient. Often it would be easier for us to do the things we try to teach our children to do. For example, it is easier, quicker and less frustrating if we dress them rather than wait while they do it for themselves. God treats us like a patient parent treats his children because He wants us to learn.

Jonah's rebellion was really a symptom of a deeper malady. The real problem was his twisted theology. This demonstrates how what we believe affects the way we behave. If we adhere to some doctrinal extreme it can restrict our ability to function as God would desire. Jonah is perplexed by what appears to him to be a confusing commission. His patriotic prejudice interpreted God's election of Israel as a rejection of all other peoples. He had a legalistic and intolerant spirit which was more inclined to malice than mercy. He was wilful and wayward. Jonah is difficult to understand and as such he is difficult to like. He does not seem to possess the evidences of grace one might expect to see adorning a servant of God in such a privileged position.

In a sense Jonah was unfit for the prophetic office, but God chose to use him. The real problem with Jonah was that he was filled with an unholy pride in Israel's status before God and an equally unholy prejudice against those outside the covenant. In his thinking grace should not extend to Gentiles.[9] Not only that, but possibly, Jonah didn't want to be the particular instrument in bringing favour to these people. He didn't want to prophesy judgement if it would not come to pass because that would make him look foolish. Jonah's reputation was at stake and he didn't want to be engaged in anything that potentially diminished his standing in the community of faith and country to which

---

[9] Nevertheless he invited the mariners to sacrifice him in order that they (heathen) might live. This shows that he had some sense of appreciation for the lives of non-Jews and that it was specifically the Ninevites whom he disliked.

he belonged. In his confession in chapter 4 Jonah clearly states that he knew God to be gracious and compassionate and from the context it is clear that he knew that God's grace applied to the people of Nineveh as well (4:2). Jonah's nationalism and the knowledge that these people would be the source of God's punishment to Israel was the real problem. Not only that, but Jonah didn't want to be the specific instrument in bringing favour to these people.

How often such thinking inhibits how God's people behave. There is a peer pressure to which church leaders, members and adherents conform because they are afraid to do anything unusual. They are afraid to step outside the box for fear of ridicule or resentment by their peers.

The incident where Jonah invites the heathen sailors to cast him overboard, in order that the crew and ship might be saved, not only demonstrates that Jonah was not a coward but it also reveals something else about the character of this man. Firstly, he did not believe that all heathen were worthless human beings and that the life of a Hebrew was worth more than the lives of several Gentiles.[10] Secondly, it shows that Jonah's real fear was focused on the idea that God could extend grace en-masse to an entirely new cohort of people. This (in his thinking) would have created an entirely different situation. There would essentially be another critical mass of people who would effectively dilute Israel's unique status. He feared that a shift in the locus of God's grace and favour on such a scale would be a step too far because it would create a new paradigm in the spiritual world.

Although Jonah was a zealous and patriotic Jewish nationalist he had compassion for these idol worshipping sailors, probably because he felt guilty that the entire situation in which they found themselves was his fault in

---

[10] This is an attitude that has a particular relevance today with regard to the ongoing Palestinian/Israeli conflict.

the first place. It could be argued that if he was not concerned about sacrificing his life he was hardly worried about his reputation. However, this argument does not take account of the reality that many men prefer their reputations to their lives. Many suicides have been committed by men who lost their jobs because they felt redundant and worthless. Many men have taken their own lives after they have lost their fortunes on the stock exchange. Many men find their dignity, status, sense of self-worth and their identities are inextricably linked to their careers.

Jonah fled because Nineveh was the capital of the Assyrian Empire and he did not want these particular people to be saved. Assyria was a dominant power in the ancient world of the Middle-East. Jonah knew that God had chosen these heathen people to chasten and discipline Israel. Other prophets of the Old Testament had predicted that the Assyrians were destined to conquer the nation of Israel.[11]

When we put ourselves in Jonah's shoes we can understand something of what he must have thought and felt. Jonah would have hoped for judgement to befall Nineveh because this would have held out the possibility of disaster being averted for Israel and Judah. He did not want to see his beloved Jerusalem destroyed or his friends, relatives and fellow citizens put to the sword. If Nineveh was destroyed then it held out the hope that Israel would be saved. This is the predicament with which Jonah was faced. There may have been some dilemma because it is unlikely that a prophet of God would refuse a commission without going through some mental anguish and soul-searching. But he made a clear choice which was rooted in his own pride and prejudice. He was unequivocal in his refusal to fulfil this commission to preach to Nineveh. He

---

[11] Hosea, Nahum and Amos foretell the destruction of Israel at the hands of the Assyrians

knew God's character very well. He knew Jehovah was merciful. He understood that if the Ninevites repented God would relent and judgement (on this barbaric people, who were destined to be the instruments of judgement on Israel and Judah) would be avoided.

Thus Jonah was given a difficult and unenviable task which no Israelite would have willingly accepted. Jonah preferred to risk incurring the wrath of God rather than being instrumental in the ultimate destruction of his own nation. This is not the action of a coward. Jonah would prefer to sacrifice himself to save his country. This would be a commendable sentiment were it not for the fact that he disobeyed God. He chose the land of God over the God of the land. His pride in his nation obstructed him from doing his spiritual duty.

In chapter 1 Jonah is fleeing from God. In chapter 2 he is praying to God. In chapter 3 he is speaking for God and in chapter 4 he is learning about God. In the first three verses of chapter 4 Jonah is displeased and dismayed that the Ninevites have repented. The prophet is perplexed by what this might mean for Israel. The prospect that prophecy (concerning the destruction of Israel at the hands of the Assyrians) would now be fulfilled deeply troubled Jonah and he did not want to be instrumental in bringing this to pass.

In chapter 4 when God asks Jonah if he has any right to be angry the prophet, astonishingly, claims that he has every right to be displeased. Some people think that the God of the *Bible*, especially the God of the Old Testament, is vengeful and volatile. But here is evidence that God is amazingly patient, merciful and gracious, not only with the Ninevites, but also with Jonah. I suspect that Jonah is not unique in this regard. We too can feel justifiably angry about certain situations rather than coming to terms with the reality of God's sovereign will. This is ultimately where the text takes us; to a place where God says that He has the right to do as He pleases.

Furthermore, God leads us to a place where He wants us to learn about His love. His grace is grand and His mercies are manifold. God wants us to see the comprehensiveness of His clemency and the wonder of His ways.

Jonah's peculiarity becomes singularly important. We should not underestimate the connection between the man and the message in *Jonah*. God has a unique job for each individual. It may not be of the same magnitude as Jonah's ministry, but it is not less meaningful in God's eyes. In chapter 9 of the novel, *Moby-Dick*[12], by Herman Melville, the chaplain onboard the whaling ship, *Pequod*, preaches a sermon[13] from *Jonah*. This ancient mariner, Mapple, climbed into the pulpit and the homily begins with the reading and singing of a 'hymn'[14]. The text is, 'Now the LORD had prepared a great fish to swallow Jonah. And Jonah was in the belly of the fish three days and three nights' (1:17). The sermon is fascinating in many ways, not least because of the powerful way it is introduced in verse form:

> The ribs and terrors in the whale,
> Arched over me in dismal gloom,
> While all God's sun-lit waves rolled by,
> And lift me deepening down to doom.
>
> I saw the opening maw of hell,
> With endless pains and sorrows there;
> Which none but they that feel can tell-
> Oh, I was plunging to despair.
>
> In black distress, I called my God,
> When I could scarce believe him mine,
> He bowed his ear to my complaints-
> No more the whale did me confine.

---

[12] Melville, Herman. *Moby-Dick*, Marshall Cavendish, 1987 (a facsimile reproduction of an edition published by Sampson Low, Marston, 1922).

[13] The title of that chapter is, 'The Sermon'.

[14] It is not, to my knowledge, really a hymn. It is a literary device constructed by Melville, himself.

> With speed he flew to my relief
> As on a radiant dolphin borne;
> Awful, yet bright as lightening shone
> The face of my deliverer God,
>
> My song for ever shall record
> That terrible, that joyful hour;
> I give the glory to my God,
> His all the mercy and the power.

The second and fifth stanzas in particular establish a connection between human experience and homiletic exposition.

There is something qualitatively different about a sermon rooted in Scripture and proven in experience. The success of preaching is difficult to measure and must be attributed to the sovereign activity of the Holy Spirit. Nevertheless it is quite likely that the perspicacity of Paul's preaching, the power of Peter's preaching and the potency of Jonah's preaching was greatly enhanced by their unique encounters with God. Jonah's life was a sermon, Paul's life was a sermon and Peter's life was a sermon.

Our lives too must be sermons. In a sense, in the Christian life, we become the message. It is not that Christianity is all about us but our lives become a story. Our faith and failure bear testimony to God. Even our scars tell stories. Many believers bear emotional scars as a result of their experiences. Many people in this world will never read the *Bible.* but they will read the lives of believers. A pure life will bear testimony to God but, ironically, a man who has failed spectacularly may be even more attractive to people who dislike piety and what they perceive as 'perfection'. They might admire people who seem to have it all together but, paradoxically, they are likely to despise them because they cannot relate to them. People want to connect with men and women whom they see as 'human' and 'approachable'. Even people within the church find the pious patriarchs in the pews somewhat intimidating and will never confide in them because they would be too ashamed. God indeed works in mysterious ways!

Mapple's sermon[15] is imaginative and insightful and whatever faults might be detected therein, Melville makes some discerning comments; not least of which is this:

> ...this book, containing only four chapters...is one of the smallest strands in the mighty cable of the Scriptures. Yet what depths of the soul does Jonah's deep sea-line sound! What a pregnant lesson to us is this prophet![16]

This indeed is a book which is relevant to the church in the twenty-first-century. Its message challenges the complacency and contemptuous attitudes of God's children towards those yet outside the precincts of pardon.

---

[15] It must be borne in mind that it is not a real sermon, though it shows a great deal of familiarity with the book of *Jonah* and the timely and timeless truths it contains. There are some things I disagree with in this text. For example, he speaks of the 'joy of Jonah' (p.36) and one would be hard pressed to find evidence of this in the book. Also he refers to Jonah as 'a coward' (p.37) and I take issue with this assumption.

[16] lc.36.

4.

Man and Message

Jonah is God's self-disclosure and as such is not primarily about Jonah, the man and prophet. Rather it is essentially about God. But Jonah is a foil that, by contrast, shows God's heart in all its magnificence.

Unlike other Old Testament prophetic books, *Jonah* is not a collection of the prophet's oracles but a narrative about the man whose heart contrasts with the heart of God. As such it is a book that is primarily about the mercy and grace of God.

Jonah is portrayed as an obstinately disobedient prophet who flees from God's clear commission to prophesy against the wickedness of the city of Nineveh. He is identified in the opening verse as the son of Amittai. This ancestry identifies him as the Jonah that is mentioned in II Kings 14: 25 who prophesied during the reign of Jeroboam II, about 785 B. C.[17]

Like the book of Ruth it presents the exclusivity of Jewish nationalism as something that does not fit with God's scheme of things. However this kind of patriotic sentiment was characteristic of the period following the reforms of Ezra and Nehemiah. Ezra, for example, had challenged

---

[17] The book, in its present form, corresponds to a much later date of composition. It was written after the Babylonian Exile (sixth century B. C.), possibly in the fifth or fourth century and certainly no later than the third century B.C. as it is numbered with the Minor Prophets in the apocryphal book of *Ecclesiasticus*, written circa 190 B.C.

the violation of God's clear command not to marry into the surrounding heathen nations once they had come into the Promised Land. He addressed the problem for what it was, an abuse of God's Word. God was, therefore, well represented in the forbidding of intermarriage with Gentiles but he was not well represented in the mistaken notion that God's gracious purposes were restricted exclusively to Israel.

Jonah in this regard is typical of the Jews of that time inasmuch as he regarded his heathen neighbours with loathing rather than love, hatred rather than hope and disgust rather than desire for their repentance. God rebukes him for his attitude. The book demonstrates that God's mercy extends to places and peoples that God's people sometimes deem worthy of damnation and even desire such an outcome!

The prophet was commissioned with a specific message for a particular people. It was a message that related to their future. Jonah was the oracle of God chosen to deliver that message. In this sense the book is prophetic. But prophecy is not exclusively about revealing future events; it is chiefly about divulging and displaying the heart and will of God.

It is important to consider the context and background of the book, failure to do this will likely result in missing the main thrust of the message. It is not only *helpful* to have some appreciation of the circumstances that led to the story that many know so well. Rather, it is *crucial* to understand the setting from which it emerges.

Jonah the Man

Every man is in some sense a product of his generation. Jonah was such a man. Consideration of Jonah the man will provide some background and introduction to the context of his life and ministry. Understanding the man is the key to unlocking the meaning of the book. There is very little factual, biographical information about him in Scripture. This dearth of detail constrains the student of this book to consider the historical setting and engage in character analysis. These, however, are not ends in themselves but means to understanding the God of history and the God of *Jonah*.

Jonah is 'the son of Amittai' (1:1). This is confirmed in 2 Kings 14:25 where the additional information is given that he came from Gath Hepher, a city that was about fifteen miles west of the sea of Galilee, close to Nazareth, and in the territory of the tribe of Zebulun, one of the Northern tribes after the kingdom of Israel had divided. This man, Jonah, exercised a prophetic ministry in the Northern kingdom somewhere around 780-755 B.C.

We have placed him in the line of the prophets, shortly after Elijah and Elisha and a little bit before Hosea and Amos. He ministered in the Northern kingdom during the reign of Jeroboam II. The separation of Israel into two kingdoms had taken place approximately two-hundred years before Jonah came on the scene. The history of the Northern ten tribes was marked by a downward spiral of spiritual decline and apostasy. The only thing that seemed to distinguish a king from his predecessor was that each successor outdid their predecessor in godlessness and wickedness.

By the time of Elijah (just before Jonah) the land had degenerated into outright apostasy and worship of the Canaanite God, Baal. The reign of Jeroboam was a time of great prosperity and success. One might expect it to be a time of great hardship and judgement but that is not so. The nation regained lost territory, expanded its borders and increased its influence. This is to be seen, not as a reward for the personal piety of Jeroboam II, who was no exception in that terrible catalogue of kings, nor is it to be seen as God turning a blind eye to people's idolatry. It was simply a gracious initiative from a merciful God. For some time God had been punishing His people because of their spiritual adultery. God had brought foreign invasions from Syria and Assyria. But the repeated defeats at the hands of their enemies had not brought the people of God to their senses or back to their God.

Jonah the Mission

Jonah is unusual among the Old Testament prophets that are recorded in Scripture. In this instance at least he is not called to preach to his own people but to a foreign nation. There are other instances of Old Testament prophets speaking against foreign nations, but they were not normally called to travel to the foreign land to proclaim the message from God. They tended to speak God's message from a distance, from their home situation. Frequently, the main purpose of the message was not only God speaking against the foreign nation but God was speaking within earshot of His own people. Part of the message was to reassure His own people of His watchfulness over them and His readiness to act on their behalf against those who oppressed them. God had a reason for not sending the prophets to enemy territory to proclaim the Word. He wanted His people to hear Him say it. But Jonah was called to go; to physically leave his own land and go to a foreign nation and deliver a specific message, not just *about* them but *to* them and *for* them.

He is called to go to Nineveh, one of the major cities of the dominant Assyrian Empire. This empire had spread its power throughout the near east and it had a reputation for unrivalled arrogance and brutality. In Isaiah God condemns Assyria as a nation and declares, "I will punish the fruit of the arrogant heart of the king of Assyria, and the glory of his haughty looks" (10:12). During Jonah's time Nineveh repented and their destruction was temporarily averted. Soon after, however, the people of Nineveh reverted to their pride, wickedness and brutality. The prophecy of Nahum is directed particularly against the city of Nineveh and generally against the nation of Assyria. Nahum describes Nineveh as a city of blood and condemns the Assyrians for their endless cruelty, wickedness, oppression, and idolatry. God will not allow such a nation to go unpunished. The fate of that tyrannical empire was determined by the sovereign God, Lord of history and all nations, because it was He who ultimately controlled their destiny. In all of its three chapters Nahum prophesied Nineveh's destruction under the hand of the Almighty. The fall of Nineveh eventually came to pass in 612 B. C.

Not only did the Assyrians have a terrible reputation for brutality but they gloried in it. In the British Museum in London today there are monuments from the Assyrian empire depicting in gory detail the atrocities that they carried out on the battlefield. They literally left fields of battle covered with slaughtered bodies. They treated their enemies with unspeakable cruelty. Contemporary Hollywood film directors would be readily supplied with an epic story of sadistic cruelty. It is not difficult to imagine how they would portray such scenes. The cameras would probably linger over a blood soaked field of mutilated bodies as far as the eye could see. But these were not imaginary scenes choreographed and refined with special effects technology for the amusement of twenty-first century audiences. Such scenes were a reality. That was the regular Assyrian way of conducting war.

One of the infamous things that they did was to fasten their victims to the ground and flay them alive! They would behead their enemies and walk away from a battlefield leaving pyramids of human heads to testify to what they were capable of doing. They had a deliberate policy of killing babies and young children simply so that they would not have to care for them in the years to come. They were among the first to pioneer the practice of deporting captured people and replacing them with foreigners. It was that policy which ultimately led to the virtual disappearance of the ten Northern tribes, just fifty years after the days of Jonah, when the Assyrians cleared the land, deported the Israelites and replaced them with other nations.

In view of all this consider how Jonah, the prophet of God was called to travel to the heartland of this godless, barbaric people, not only with a message of judgement but also the prospect of that judgement being averted if they should repent.

These were the very people who were threatening to destroy Israel. They were Israel's number one enemy and Jonah is told to go to them. It is like somebody in New York City after 11 September, 2001 who had family members, friends and fellow countrymen killed in the destruction of the 'Twin Towers' being instructed by God to go to Afghanistan and seek out Osama Ben Laden and preach to him the gospel of salvation. It's like a mother in Jerusalem cradling the shattered body of her son who has been blown up in a Palestinian suicide bomb attack and in the midst of that carnage imagine God saying to her, go to the headquarters of the Palestinian authority and speak of a God of mercy. Consider God saying to some Jewish person in Hitler's day to go to the headquarters of the Third Reich and speak of a God of love and forgiveness. The commission entrusted to Jonah is of that kind.

This book is not just about a man named Jonah who is idle, disobedient and indifferent, declining a particular job. Here was a man who instinctively detested the prospect of the Ninevites being spared God's wrath. He would have preferred God to destroy them without giving them any warning because inherent in such a warning was the possibility of the Ninevites availing of God's mercy through repentance. Jonah is having difficulty not just in *complying* with the commission entrusted to him by God, but in *comprehending* the idea that he should go to Nineveh and thereby open the door of mercy to these heathen. He was not interested in the idea that these 'savages' could possibly become peaceful neighbours and the consequent benefits accruing from that to Israel.[18] It seems he would rather they be destroyed.

Jonah is sometimes dismissed as a pathetic, apathetic and idle person or as a recalcitrant individual. Certainly he was obstinately disobedient to God's clear instructions. But he was far from being indifferent about the fate of the Ninevites. Jonah is sometimes presented as a coward, but there is evidence in this book that he was not easily frightened and that he did not lack courage. Yes he was called to go to the most sadistic, cruel people of his day. The people who were threatening to destroy his nation, and within fifty years would do so. He was to go to this people and announce a message of judgement which held out the contingent possibility of forgiveness and mercy. His major problem was not apathy, indolence or cowardice; rather it was a patriotic sense of pride and an unambiguous prejudice against the Ninevites.

Jonah: The Message

What is the message of this book? What is the point of its inclusion in the canon of Scripture? The liberal theologian would say it is just a parable, a story invented to convey some truth about the Word of God or the love of God. Perhaps some people think that it is a great example of cross cultural mission where God calls a person from one culture to go into another. That is certainly an interesting dimension to the book but it is not the central theme. The primary focus and value of *Jonah* is God! This book is a

---

[18] Any such benefits would be relatively short term and would last little more than a generation, though Jonah would not have known how long peace might prevail.

tremendous character study of the person and attributes of God. It is not merely a character study of the man Jonah. Certainly there is much we can learn about Jonah. Although the pride and prejudice of Jonah may be explored in depth, such analysis functions ultimately to show, by contrast, the essential nature of God. The juxtaposition of Jonah and God in dialogue and deeds serves to portray the divine nature so that the reader may become better acquainted with the deity.

Without doubt the idea of disobedience and its consequences is relevant to any careful study of the book but that is not what *Jonah* is primarily about. This book shows how God deals with individuals and nations, those that are His own and those who do not own Him as their God. It presents God as magnanimous in mercy, longsuffering in love and great in grace. It reveals Him in all the regal splendour of His majestic, sovereign power over empires, oceans and their occupants. God is seen as an astonishingly patient parent with the petulant and pouting prophet.

The sovereignty of God is another great theme emphasised in this book. Chapter 1 reveals something of God's sovereignty. The ways of the Almighty are not always easy to discern, in fact they are sometimes impossible to understand. But it is comforting to know that He knows what He is doing, that He is omnipotent and omniscient. It is this all-powerful and all-knowing God who sent a preacher to Nineveh.

God says, "Arise, go to Nineveh…" "Arise" means get yourself into a position whereby you can take the necessary action. It means to get up from lying or sitting. So whatever Jonah was doing at the exact time of this commission (sleeping, eating a meal…) he was to rise above whatever occupied or preoccupied him. He was to rise above his feelings and the difficulties of the task and assume a position of readiness to proceed, and in the strength of God know the power of the Almighty which was equal to the charge.

It was the signal to be on his mark, like the athlete awaiting the starting pistol; to be in readiness (and if necessary to make preparation) for action. We might well ask what preoccupies us and what prevents us from bring the message of the gospel to lost souls. Are we making preparations, are we in a state of readiness and willingness and availability to go to others with this word from God? Let us set aside the things that hinder and beset us so that we may be unencumbered in obedience.

God said, "Arise, go to Nineveh, that great city, and cry out against it; for their wickedness has come up before Me" (1:2). There are many accounts in Old Testament writing where the Word of the Lord was heard by individuals. In every other instance in the Old Testament where the Word of the Lord was received the messenger responded accordingly. When the sovereign God called the servant answered and when He instructed the servant obeyed. What the sovereign commanded them to proclaim they proclaimed; but this is not so with Jonah. This is an unparalleled act of insubordination. God said, "go", and Jonah effectively said "no" in the way he responded. God said go East to Nineveh and Jonah defiantly went West, to Joppa where he boarded a ship bound for Tarshish.

Jonah could have stayed where he was but he decided to travel to Tarshish. He did not go in the general direction of Nineveh and stop short, rather he went in the opposite direction! This is not just a failure to complete a mission, it is a refusal to commence it. It is not that he tried to obey but balked before fulfilling his commission. It is clear from his behaviour that he had absolutely no intention whatsoever of complying with the expressed will of God. It is astonishing to behold how God tolerates such impertinence.

Joppa is the only natural harbour on Israel's Mediterranean coast. It is about thirty-three miles west of Jerusalem. There he found a ship bound for Tarshish, which is in Spain. The word 'Tarshish' is used three times in 1:3.

Obviously, the point is being stressed that Jonah is not going to Nineveh but to Tarshish, a distant city in the opposite direction. We have noted earlier that Jonah decided to go where the God of Israel, the true God, was not known, where God's covenant with Israel was not acknowledged. He was determined to locate himself in a society that knew nothing of God's Word ministered through prophet and psalmist. We noted that Jonah is wilfully going as far away as he can from the place where God dwelt with His people. We noted, in short, that he was determined to flee the very presence of God. We noted that he suppressed his belief in the Scriptures (that he knew so well) which spoke of the omnipresence of the Almighty and the futility of trying to escape His presence by geographical relocation.[19] But now he was about to test it and find it true in his own experience, like many other wayward people of God.

The Scriptures here in the original language use Jewish imagery where Jonah's vain attempt to run from God is conveyed in terms of descent. In 1:3, for example, it is noticeable that the text says he went 'down' to Joppa. In the same verse, it says, he went 'down' into the ship. Verse 5 contains the statement that Jonah, 'had gone down into the lowest parts of the ship'. This is intentional Jewish imagery calculated to indicate that downward is away from God. This is a mark of spiritual decline.

Running away was Jonah's way of declining the commission from God. It is recorded that Jeroboam II, 'restored the territory of Israel from the entrance of Hamath to the Sea of the Arabah, according to the word of the LORD God of Israel, which He had spoken through His servant Jonah the son of Amittai, the prophet who *was* from

---

[19] Jonah knew his Old Testament Scriptures very well indeed and it is unlikely that he was unaware of the idea of the omnipresence of God. Clearly he did know Psalm 139 (this becomes evident later on in the narrative) and this psalm teaches that it is impossible to escape the presence of God.

Gath Hepher' (2 Kings 14:25). That passage goes on to say that the Lord saved Israel by the hand of this king (v.27). One of his military achievements was the recovery of Damascus and Hamath for Israel (v.28). This restoration is presented as God's faithfulness to His covenant promise with Israel. The covenant involved the preservation of the people of Israel in perpetuity and the possession of territory. Thus whenever Israel was punished for their rebelliousness to God they were led captive to foreign territory. Jonah had a prophetic ministry that proclaimed prosperity in covenant terms (restoration of territory) to Israel. In spite of the fact that Jeroboam II was a sinful king (v.24) God was merciful to His suffering people and granted relief. It is likely that Jonah was appreciated for his favourable message to Israel.

In view of this his commission to go to Nineveh with a message of judgement (which was implicitly contingent on their refusal to repent) opened the possibility of repentance and forgiveness for Israel's enemy. The possibility that God would spare these people rather than destroy them meant that they would continue to be a threat to the peace and prosperity of Israel. Jonah knew that Israel could not ultimately thrive while co-existing with the Ninevites. The idea that God would treat such people favourably by staying His judgement was repulsive to Jonah because he was deeply prejudiced.

His preconceived opinion was that God was on Israel's side and would defend the nation against her enemies. In his view the covenant had nothing to do with heathen nations. It meant that Israel was exclusively favoured by God. Like his contemporaries he overlooked the universal significance of the covenant promise made initially to Abram. The terms of that covenant were not only that God would make a nation of Abram's seed but, also that through him all nations would be blessed.

Jonah is so completely disgusted by his task that he defiantly registers his protest by going to a place where there will not be ubiquitous reminders of the presence of God. If he was trying to run from the presence of God it was as foolish as Adam and Eve hiding behind a bush and thinking that would be sufficient to conceal them from God's sight. Staying where he was would have constituted *resistance* to God's command but running outside the covenant territory constituted *rebellion* and shows the depth of the loathing in Jonah's heart for the Ninevites.

So initially, God sent a preacher and then God sent a storm. In this it is evident that God retains authority over His inanimate creation and can intervene to control these elemental forces at will to suit His purposes. This may bring to mind the occasion when the disciples were travelling in a boat with Jesus and a storm arose which threatened to capsize the vessel. The fearful disciples woke Jesus who was asleep. Christ had been preaching all day, from the boat, to a great multitude gathered along the shore. It is noteworthy that Jesus commanded the winds to cease and the sea to be calm and at His word the storm immediately stopped. This terrified the disciples who wondered who He was that even the wind and the seas obeyed Him. They had seen His authority over sickness when he cured a leper. They had witnessed His authority to restore sight to the blind, heal the deaf, make the lame to walk again, cure a woman who was bleeding for twelve years. They marvelled at His authority to forgive sin and to raise the dead. These things were sufficient evidence of His divinity, but it took this incident in the boat to enable the disciples to get a glimpse of His unlimited power over nature. They were terrified of the one they knew so well because for a brief moment they realised they were in the presence of the deity Himself. The disciples observed that the wind and the seas obey Him. Jonah, the chosen prophet of God was disobedient but the wind and the seas obeyed. It was easier for God to control these great forces than to get the cooperation of His servant preacher.

Jonah was on the run but discovering that he could not get away from God, the doctrine of God's omnipresence came alive in his experience. God hurled this storm upon the sea. It is the same word as that used in verse 1:5 to refer to throwing the cargo into the sea. It is again used about throwing Jonah into the sea. This was not a natural storm. This was God throwing a storm. God hurled this storm into Jonah's life to teach him a lesson and to get His way in Jonah's life. God was exercising His sovereign control over the physical elements and also orchestrating events in Jonah's life that would bring him to the point of compliance with the divine will.

The reader will observe that Jonah was asleep below deck while this storm was raging. The charitable interpretation would be simply that he was exhausted after his journey to Joppa and fell into a deep sleep and was completely unaware of the tempest raging all around. A more critical interpretation would suggest that he was snug because he was smug! He was self-satisfied and content in his present position and not only unaware of the traumatic circumstances of the crew but unconcerned about their plight.

Jonah is in this situation because he is in deliberate rebellion against God. He disobeyed the unambiguous instructions of God. Everything seemed to be fine up to a point. He fled to Joppa looking for a way to escape and conveniently located a ship going to Tarshish. He paid the fare and boarded the ship. The Israelites were not naturally a seafaring people and travelled overland wherever possible as they had an aversion to the sea. Boarding the ship reveals Jonah's resolve to flee. He had resolved in his heart not to preach in Nineveh and demonstrated a dogged determination to distance himself as far as possible from any possibility of fulfilling that responsibility.

Jonah's Complacency

He went below deck and fell into a deep sleep. He continues to sleep soundly while the storm is tossing the ship about on the sea, unaware of the imminent danger that the ship might sink. The waves were such that the vessel was creaking under the strain. Jonah at this point in the narrative could not be more complacent about the circumstances surrounding him. It is true that he was asleep, but it is equally true that he was not alert to the fact that he was the cause of putting the crew in mortal peril. One of the salutary lessons to be derived from this account of Jonah's situation is that it is possible for the Christian to be out of the will of God and yet have a false sense of security. Is it possible to be at ease when there is danger all around? Is it possible to be at ease when there is work to be done? Is it possible to be at ease even though lives are at risk? One of the most ominous warnings in Scripture is not against unbelievers but against believers: 'Woe to those who are at ease in Zion' (Amos 6:1).

The Sailors' Concern

Jonah's complacency contrasts dramatically with the sailors' concern. They are conspicuously active whereas he is remarkably inactive. In verse 1:6 it says; 'So the captain came to him, and said to him, "What do you mean, sleeper?" The captain is astonished that Jonah was asleep and asked Jonah to get up, and call on his god! The contrast is inescapably stark and draws attention to the irony of the situation, where a pagan feels compelled to urge God's prophet to engage in intercessory prayer!

The sailors are concerned about the nature and purpose of the storm. They are superstitious and in a sense 'god-fearing' men. They did not have knowledge of the true God but they had a sense of eternity in their hearts. Even though they worshipped false gods they nevertheless discerned something was wrong and that this storm had a supernatural significance. How they could know the difference between a natural storm and a supernatural one which indicated that deity needed to be appeased is not clear. Seafarers are notoriously superstitious even today, but at that time and in that place there was a greater superstition. The passage says, 'All the sailors were afraid and each cried out to his own god' (1:5). They understood that somebody on board was responsible for the catastrophe and they cast lots as a means of finding out who was to blame and this procedure identified Jonah as the culprit (1:7). They ask a series of questions to ascertain the nature of the problem (1:8). The word used for 'trouble' is a translation of the word 'evil'.

These men perceive that this was not a natural phenomenon. They understand the storm to be a malevolent force with some spiritual significance. This is a storm brought on by an offended deity. So they resorted to the ancient custom of casting lots to find out who it was. Every god or goddess was connected to a specific place or particular people. So in order to find out who was causing the trouble they had to find out what offended the deity. This is the reason for the barrage of questions in verse 1:8. They want to know if Jonah is the cause of their difficulties.

While Jonah was slumbering the sailors were desperately anxious about the spiritual dimension of their difficulties. They were also concerned about Jonah's life. These pagan people, tough and skilled sailors, display a significant measure of care for Jonah. They could have suggested throwing him overboard in order to get out of danger. But they make a heroic effort to preserve his life. They show a great reluctance to comply with Jonah's request to be thrown overboard. Instead they attempt to row back to land, but were unable to do so, because the storm grew wilder. These heathen sailors reveal more compassion for the life of the rebellious servant of God than Jonah ever showed for the people of Nineveh. Here is a shame that must be confessed, that there are of other faiths people who in their attitudes and actions outshine Christians.

Jonah's Confession

Jonah was exposed as the guilty party. It is remarkable that God used godless-people and practices to bring His truth to the surface. The prophet made a frank disclosure of his culpability and accountability. He declared that his God is not merely a tribal deity with limited jurisdiction. He confessed that he worships the God of heaven, who made the sea and the land. Perhaps this was Jonah's way of acknowledging the fact that he owed Jehovah homage. But the reality is that he was not paying due honour to his God. Worship involves reverence and obedience, but Jonah is irreverent and disobedient.

Jonah could have repented and disembarked at the next port to return to his mission in Nineveh. If somebody offends God he can either, repent and put his life in order by getting back on track or accept the punishment that sin merits. Jonah knew how to appease God. He had the choice to repent or face possible death and he opted for the latter. Jonah knew that he could not evade God's chastisement but he would rather die than go to Nineveh. Three times in this brief book of Jonah he said he would rather die than see those people saved. It is a shocking thought. God sent a preacher, God sent a storm and then God sent a fish. The sailors realised that they would all drown if they did not agree to Jonah's request, so finally, as a last resort, and very reluctantly they threw Jonah overboard.

Jonah had walked away from God by turning his back on his calling and commission. Although he rejected the ministry that had been given to him, God had not rejected Jonah. God had not yet finished with Jonah and in His sovereignty he decided to preserve the prophet. It is amazing that God would want to give this pathetic failure another opportunity to fulfil his prophetic ministry to preach in

Nineveh. Such is the character of God and His astounding grace. All who serve Him must be grateful that He does not fail those who fail Him. Reading the book of *Jonah* will cause even the haughty head to bow and the hardened heart to be humbled. The reader is overwhelmed with amazement and wonder that God deals with His servants so graciously and patiently.

The hearts of those who are called of God and commissioned with the task of preaching the gospel may grow complacent and cold. This may be reflected in disinterest, dissatisfaction and disobedience. Preachers are not necessarily the super-saints that they may be supposed to be and can, like any other child of God, be prone to wander from His ways. There are few today who would not give up on people of such waywardness and wash their hands of them. Even the best of God's servants are frail and flawed individuals and some are even prone to foolishness. Yet God does not forsake His children. He does not give up; He has plans for His people. It is through them that His purposes will be fulfilled. His grand designs will be accomplished and never thwarted.

An honest examination of the wayward Jonah will reveal some wrong attitudes, but as the old adage says: 'those who live in glass-houses should not throw stones'. For this reason the believer should be slow to point an accusing finger at him and swift to examine oneself. For who can say that he has no need to be more receptive and responsive to God's Word? Exploring this book can enable the Christian to get to know the heart of God better and marvel at His grace and power. It can also help believers to get better acquainted with themselves. The eyes of its readers ought to look beyond the sacred page to seek the Lord's will. The believer must not merely want a better grasp of the text or a better intellectual understanding of the truth. These things in themselves will yield only limited benefit. The most profitable approach to *Jonah* is to have a sincere desire to know God better and be more like Him in attitude and action.

God provided a great fish. This is the inspired, infallible, inerrant and authoritative Word of the living God and is neither legend nor fable nor parable. The Christian has cause to rejoice in his privileged access to Scripture as it discloses the mind, heart and will of the sovereign God. It is wonderful that God in His graciousness has not left His people to grope in the dark in order to find the path that pleases Him. Christians don't have to invent a code of conduct through trial and error. God has given clear the most vicious, pitiless and ruthless people on the planet, and he was expected to preach a message not only of judgement but of repentance and forgiveness to them.

It has been proposed that Jonah was not a coward; that he was not afraid to die; he did not count his life to be of superior value to the heathen crewmen and that this is evident in his willingness to allow himself to be thrown overboard in order to save the ship and crew. This act may be seen as a perverse attempt to appease God but it is nonetheless favourable toward the sailors. He is not prejudiced against heathen per se. But he sees them as people outside God's covenant community. He can relate to them on such terms but he has major difficulty with the possibility that such brutal people as the Ninevites, who had the potential to destroy Israel, could be brought within God's sphere of grace. The thought that such a nation would be preserved presented the very real potential of Israel's destruction. This was anathema to Jonah. It is so detestable to him that every fibre of his being refuses to go along with it.

A few years ago my wife was teaching *Jonah* in Sunday-School. She told me afterwards that the children really enjoyed the idea that the fish did what God told him to do, but Jonah did not do what God had instructed him to do! The notion that the fish was more obedient than the prophet may be amusing, but it is also sad that the human species is so wayward. God who, in His supreme power and authority, sent Jonah and launched the storm also provided the miraculous means to rescue the unwilling prophet and prepare him for conformity to His will. In doing this God was teaching Jonah a valuable lesson that no matter what effort he made he could not avoid God's purposes for him. He could flee to the most remote location but that would not hinder the Almighty from ultimately seeing His divine will accomplished.

5.

Saturated in Scripture

It is a curious thing that Jonah (though a Hebrew) took a longer, more indirect and dangerous journey by sea, by going to Joppa and boarding a ship bound for the port of Tarshish, when he could have taken a shorter, safer and less arduous overland journey to Nineveh.

Hebrew literature portrays water as a potent symbol of peril, despair and death. So to plummet into the waters was not only an overwhelming physical encounter with the awesome power of the sea; it was also a spiritual experience; to penetrate the dominion of death. Sheol was the murky and mysterious realm of departure from the world without any prospect of return. For Jonah the idea of death by drowning would have held an appalling vista of terrors. Yet he faces this with great courage. To be slaughtered by the Ninevites would, possibly, have been a less fearful prospect. He is wiling to be cast overboard in order to save the ship and its heathen crew. Surely this is an evidence that Jonah was neither a coward nor a bigot!

There is a tendency for people to ignore chapter 2. The rest of the story intrigues the reader: Jonah fleeing God, the dramatic storm, the re-commissioning of the prophet, the repentance of the Ninevites, Jonah sitting under the shade of the gourd and his moody dialogue with God. But one is inclined to merely glance at chapter 2. However, the subsequent chapters occur only because of what takes place in chapter 2. It is important, therefore to examine this chapter.

In spite of the fact that Jonah had tried to distance himself from God he found himself in circumstances controlled and orchestrated by the Almighty. He is rescued by the Lord who provided a great fish. Enveloped in this unimaginable place with the pungent odour of semi-digested food, in total darkness, Jonah cried out to God. It is from that most peculiar location that the prophet/preacher began to communicate with God. God kept Jonah not only alive but conscious so that he was capable of communing with Him. In that solitary and strange place he had time to contemplate all that had taken place. God had miraculously intervened in the events of his life and as he reflected on that 'salvation' his spirit yielded to God in prayer.

It was a supremely Scriptural prayer with numerous allusions to and quotes from the Psalms, especially. In fact the prayer is so saturated in the Psalms that some liberal theologians have suggested that the second chapter of Jonah and maybe the entire book was composed at a considerably later date than the events recorded in these four chapters. The reason for this speculation is merely incredulity that Jonah could have been so familiar with so many portions of Scripture. Yet, in prayer meetings today one frequently hears the saints pray the Scriptures in such a way. Many mature believers, having spent a lifetime reading the Word and listening to it being preached have become very familiar with it. In childhood many people committed large portions of it to memory and are able to recall it even in old age. Considering the fact that Jonah is a preacher and prophet of God it is not at all unusual that he would exhibit a profound familiarity with the Psalms. The Old Testament writings, particularly the Psalms, had permeated his way of thinking and he could retrieve it at will from his mind. This would have been particularly so in an oral age when there was nothing unusual in people memorising great epic sagas, Like Homer's *Iliad* and *Odyssey* and passed them from one generation to the next until they were finally written down. Even today in Christian churches in Eastern Europe young people are taught to memorise lengthy passages of Scripture. It is not unusual to hear children recite an entire book of the *Bible* for a Sunday-School award ceremony.[20]

In difficulty and danger Jonah turned to the Word of God. Often God's people in distressing situations experience difficulty in finding words that adequately articulate the trauma of their souls. In such circumstances God's Word or a cherished hymn (frequently based on Scripture) can be the vehicle for conveying their emotions. In this way the Psalms provide a safe space for exploring and explaining the turmoil of the soul. They give perspective and shape to prayer. The anguish and yearnings of the heart may be more readily expressed in the great Hebrew hymn book of the Old Testament. There in the maw of that great fish Jonah expressed the substance of his thoughts in the poetic style of the Psalms. When human words seem inadequate God's Word seems appropriate. The Psalms are a great comfort to God's people at such times.

Sometimes the believer may approach Scripture with a cold heart, as a regular discipline but soon the heart thaws. The heart quickly warms to the Psalms which are wonderfully devotional; they engage the mind, frame the emotions and stimulate the will.

Jonah remembered the Scriptures he had meditated upon in the past so that even in that dark and strange place the Word of God ministered his soul. He could recall only what he had committed to memory. Jonah's prayer was rich in allusions to and quotations from the Psalms and

---

[20] It is more likely that a New Testament book like *Romans* or *Hebrews* will be chosen for memorisation. The book of *Romans* contains 16 chapters of solid theology and no narrative and Hebrews has 13 equally substantial chapters of profound teaching. Frankly this puts us in the West to shame!

other parts of Scripture. Even when he was not quoting verbatim from the Word his style of expression resonated with the idioms of Scripture so that his language echoed the Psalms.

Many saints who have been imprisoned for their faith and deprived of their Bibles have found nourishment and comfort for their souls in retrieving such treasure from their hearts. Often they have had to commit Scripture to memory because they either did not own a Bible or they anticipated a time of incarceration where they would not be allowed to peruse the Scriptures. Sadly, committing Scripture to memory is a practice that has fallen into abeyance in many Western churches today. It is something that can and should be revived. Children's talks which use object lessons and stories with a moral emphasis have their place in church life but memorising Scripture should not be displaced.

There may be times when we feel unable to utter words that adequately convey the turmoil or pain we feel. There may be days, perhaps, when the weakness of our bodies or the torments of our minds prevents us from composing a coherent prayer. There may be occasions when our minds are clouded by confusion and doubt. It is at such times that Scripture enables us to enunciate these inner conflicts in prayer. An issue facing the church today is biblical literacy. Many Christians are not very interested in preaching or reading and as a consequence they do not know the Word of God in the way that previous generations knew it. This should be a matter of grave concern especially when even those who have had a theological training are not as familiar with the Scriptures as one might expect.

There are dark days in the lives of all believers and it is at such times that they need to have something in reserve. One of the reasons for the decline in the discipline of memorising Scripture is the availability of numerous versions of the *Bible*. Some will say that it is a great blessing to have many translations available to us whereas others will disagree. However, one problem arising from different translations is that it leads to confusion. We do not wish to enter a debate about versions of the *Bible* but it seems clear that the Authorised Version (which is a literal translation) lends itself very well to memorisation. The Jacobean English has a cadence that is almost poetic. Whereas, for example, the New International Version (which is not a literal translation but a dynamic equivalent), is more prosaic. Some will suggest the N.I.V. is clearer because it does not have antiquated expressions and obsolete words but few would deny that it is more difficult to memorise.

So Jonah's prayer is beautifully biblical but it is also profoundly personal. In the eight short verses of actual prayer within this chapter the personal pronoun is used more than twenty times. This is not necessarily a bad thing; in fact it is quite understandable under the circumstances. However, if we consider his prayer in the light of this it reveals something significant about this man. Jonah is very much aware of his relationship with God. In the opening verse of chapter 2 it is stated that Jonah prayed to the Lord *his* God. Not 'the Lord God'. The text here emphasises the fact that Jonah has a relationship with God. Yet it is a self-centred prayer. He is naturally concerned about his circumstances and, as one might expect, this is the focus of his prayer.

The Peril of Personal Prayer

In times of difficulty it is normal for our prayers to be shaped by our problem. The perspective of prayer will naturally be influenced by our circumstances. However, there is a potential problem inherent in this kind of prayer. The danger is that our prayer lives will become preoccupied with the problem to the point of becoming self-centred. Then we approach the Bible with a similar attitude, looking for that personal word of prophecy about what the future has in store for us. Of course we should read the Word with a sense of expectancy that God will have something to say to us personally. But to use it as a lucky dip or horoscope is to abuse it. We need to see the big picture.

Jonah's prayer is both profoundly Scriptural and acutely personal. Here the prophet of God sees a number of distinct dimensions and facets. Firstly, Jonah mentions, in his prayer, 'The Gates of Death'. This vivid image expresses the devastating feeling of despair that Jonah felt as he sank in the surging sea and was swallowed by a great fish.

In order to gain a fuller appreciation of the potency of this imagery it is helpful to know something of the Hebrew perception of the cosmos. Hebrews believed that the universe consisted of three strata: Heaven, Earth and Sheol. Heaven was thought to be spatially above planet earth. They supposed the earth was buoyed on subterranean waters, secured by supporting columns and anchored by mountains. For the Hebrew, Sheol was the sphere of the dead and it was imagined that it existed as a region beneath the earth. They did not understand the sea as people do today. Undoubtedly, the sea was used by Hebrews for fishing and perhaps, reluctantly for travel. Nevertheless, they had a primeval fear of the seas and oceans which is reflected in Hebrew writings of the period. In the popular Hebrew imagination the deep was always connected with darkness and death. The Hebrew world-view would have had a profound influence in shaping his understanding of his experience.

Jonah's prayer is personal, profound and passionate. We have said that the language of his prayer demonstrates a familiarity with the psalms but we should also note that the psalms often convey the idea of great trouble as drowning, but not in the physical sense of being submerged in water.

Here are some examples that represent merely a brief glance at such language: 'He sent from above, He took me; He drew me out of many waters' (Ps.18:16). 'Save me, O God!

For the waters have come up to *my* neck. I sink in deep mire, where *there is* no standing; I have come into deep waters, where the floods overflow me' (Ps.69:1-2). 'Deliver me out of the mire, and let me not sink; let me be delivered from those who hate me, and out of the deep waters. Let not the floodwater overflow me, nor let the deep swallow me up; and let not the pit shut its mouth on me' (Ps.69:14-15). 'You have afflicted *me* with all Your waves (Ps.88:7). 'Then the waters would have overwhelmed us, The stream would have gone over our soul; Then the swollen waters would have gone over our soul' (Ps.124:4-5). 'Stretch out Your hand from above; rescue me and deliver me out of great waters' (Ps.144:7). These selected verses express the thought that the Hebrew worldview was influenced by the idea that there was a pit of death beneath the sea.

An awareness of this facilitates a sympathetic reading of the first six verses of Jonah's prayer in chapter 2. More than that, however, is the impression it leaves on the heart of the reader as he senses the despair in the heart of this man. Jonah is a man who goes beyond the emotions of physical drowning to lay bare a soul that feels he is drowning spiritually. He mentions 'the moorings of the mountains' (v.6) which conveys the idea that Jonah feels he is plummeting to the very roots of the universe. This is not only the deepest and darkest physical location but also the realm of spiritual darkness. In other words, the prophet hits rock-bottom.

The idea being stressed is that it is not possible to go any lower. In 2:6 Jonah refers to feeling that: 'The earth with its bars *closed* behind me forever'. This is typical of the contemporary Hebrew imagery of Sheol as the subterranean world, which is compared to a stronghold with a fortified gateway denying any possibility of egress. Entering that sphere was a one-way journey as the gates would be shut to imprison those admitted, forever. Jonah had the feeling of being locked up in this nether world. He is at the lowest point possible, not just in a literal and physical sense (and certainly not in a merely metaphorical sense), but emotionally and spiritually he is shut up to a world of despair. Although the psalmists and other Old Testament writers used this language allegorically to describe their misery, anguish and desolation; for Jonah this was also a shocking physical reality. So the situation he depicts is not just symbolic of his despondency it was actually his reality.

In this prayer Jonah says, 'I have been cast out of Your sight' (v.4). As he is speaking directly to God it obviously means that he feels exiled from God's sovereign and watchful care. He followed the route of rebellious disobedience and this is where it led. But this is not his ultimate destination. Perhaps it is tempting to think that this is what Jonah wanted. He sought to run away from God and desired to go to a place where God's name was not known and His Word was not spoken.

There is a great caution here for all who serve God and that is to desire only what God deems best for us. Many Christians struggle with what is often called 'unanswered prayer'. However, there is a similar and perhaps worse difficulty; the problem of 'answered prayer'. One of the most disturbing statements in God's Word is that God 'gave them their request but sent leanness into their soul (Ps.106:14-15). God's people should be careful about what they want and especially about what they request of God in prayer.

In his failed endeavour to run away from God Jonah sees the gates of death but he also sees the sovereign activity of God. He is completely certain that he has come to be in the belly of this big fish by God's design and that it is a direct result of attempting to flee from God in disobedience. This is evident from the confession he makes to the heathen sailors, 'the men knew that he fled from the presence of the LORD, because he had told them' (1:10b). It is likewise obvious that he does not blame the ship's crew for his circumstances. He is conscious that God is ultimately in control of his situation and in his prayer he acknowledges this awareness and attributes his casting into the sea to God: 'You cast me into the deep, into the heart of the seas' (2:3). Jonah acknowledges the sovereign hand of God in his life.

This man, in spite of his failings has a solid basis to his faith. He sees God's hand even in the darkest experience of his life. Here is a tremendous challenge for every believer, to know that God is in control and that He is nearby in whatever strange circumstances we may find ourselves. There is a great solace in resting in the sovereign will of God. Here we find a maturity of faith in a person who is often deemed to be no more than an object lesson about disobedience.

Certainty of God's sovereign will confirms our faith and consoles our hearts in times of distress. It is here that the believer finds comfort and a calm confidence in minor and major matters. There is immense tranquillity and serenity in having such an understanding at the core of one's faith. How easy it is to believe when all is well, but it is challenging to trust in this glorious doctrine when all appears to have gone wrong. There may be times in the lives of believers when every door seems closed. When one feels trapped and alone in a dungeon of despair, faith in God's sovereignty can bring light and peace even to the darkest place in a believer's experience. An unconditional conviction in the sovereignty of God overrules the troubles, frustrations, difficulties and disappointments of life.

Job is an individual who relied completely on the sovereignty of God. He acknowledged that God had control of all the circumstances of his life. He lacked nothing in wealth and wellbeing. He had a family, a farm and friends. More than all of that, he had an unshakeable faith in God, which was based on a proper understanding of the nature of the divine character. There was patent proof of God's blessing in his life. That sacred sign of God's favour seemed to turn dramatically into sovereign sanction of the calamity and catastrophe that fell upon him until he had nothing. His world disintegrated. It is instructive to consider Job's response. He says 'the Lord gave and the Lord has taken away'. He did not think of his tragic situation as the victory of his adversaries. His perception excluded the Sibeans and the Chaldeans from the root cause of his ruin. He did not blame his misfortune on the indiscriminate and unpredictable fire from heaven. He did not see the desert wind as the source of the disaster that had befallen him. Rather he attributes his downfall to the Lord, and readily recognises God's right to give and to take away. Although he remonstrates with the Lord, there is no tone of recrimination in his reaction to the calamities in his life.

Job proceeds to pronounce something exceptionally noteworthy: 'May the name of the Lord be praised'. The sovereignty of God is a wonderful theme and the contemplation of it can never be exhausted or adequately expressed. It has rich seams of treasure which the believer can mine to enrich his spiritual life and the lives of others. Christians may speak fluently and sing fervently about the sovereignty of God, but this magnificent Scriptural truth is frequently professed in speech and song in a glib manner. When the believer encounters some disappointment how often he becomes dissatisfied, displeased, distressed, discontent, disenchanted and disillusioned. Trials and tragedies are part of life and even those who profess to believe in the sovereignty of God may in times of tribulation contradict this principle doctrine by showing a lack of confidence in God's sovereign control. Sadly we are prone to doubt God and distrust His wisdom, power, love and control. Some, in their distress, will even dare to question God and accuse Him of indifference and cruelty. 'Why have you not watched over me? Are there limits in your power to control events? Why did you allow such a thing to occur?'

We are all prone to charge God with mismanagement and negligence. In certain traumatic situations we try to blame somebody and sadly, may even point an accusing finger at the sovereign God.

Imprisoned in the belly of this great fish Jonah fears that his life is coming to an ignoble end. Yet in his distress he accepts that God has ordained that it should be so. He is not reproaching God; rather he is acknowledging his trust in the sovereignty of God. Although he saw the gates of death he believed that God was orchestrating events in accordance with the council of His own will. We must give Jonah credit for such confidence in God, considering the extraordinary circumstances in which he found himself.

Jonah does not complain about his situation He states that he has been banished from the sight of God. In this he declares his guilt. Then he says that he will look again towards God's holy temple (v.4). In saying this he has clearly determined to depend upon God's sovereign intervention. Jonah has fresh faith that God, who has already intervened in providing the great fish, will rescue and restore him to intimate communion and his irrevocable commission. He appreciates that the God who rescued him in this miraculous way is going to renew his life and ministry, 'I will look again towards Your holy temple' (v.4). These words resound with the certainty of faith.

For a Jew looking toward the temple is an act of faith in which he orients his soul toward his covenant God. He believes that even in such a place God hears the anguished prayers of His people and helps. He looks toward the temple in his memory and imagination in order to remind himself of God's promise to protect and preserve His people. The temple symbolised the presence of the living God among His covenant people. He humbly appeals to the pledge made to Solomon many years previously at the dedication of the temple in Jerusalem. So his look toward the temple is a request to benefit from the specific promise made by God to Solomon. Several times in Solomon's prayer to God and in God's answer to Solomon we have the promise that, 'when my people in distress or in exile look towards this place I will hear from Heaven and I will answer them'.

Jonah had become estranged from God because of his disobedience. Now by faith he sees the temple in Jerusalem. He is rapidly renewed in faith and hope. Jonah is not engaging in some superstitious exercise or religious ritual. In looking toward the temple he is remembering God's promise of help in times of distress and also seeing the temple as the place where God dwelt among His people. Jonah is petitioning God to apply that promise. So he says, "When my life was fainting away, I remembered the LORD, and my prayer came to you, into your holy temple" (2:7). He is declaring his faith in God. The word 'remembered' in this context does not simply mean that he recalled to his mind some thoughts about the temple. Remembering in this sense is not merely retrieving something from the recesses of one's mind and is not the opposite of 'forgetting'. The *Bible* frequently uses the word 'remembering' for action established on prior obligation. So in remembering, Jonah is effectively determining to act upon his previous commitment to function as God's messenger.

In the human realm forgetfulness is a weakness. How true it is that people remember the things they should forget and forget the things they should remember. However, with God, forgetting is a conscious act that demonstrates His power. It is not, therefore a weakness but a strength which demonstrates His divine otherness. Sometimes, no matter how hard we try; the things we want to remember we forget and the things we want to forget we remember. That is because we are frail and feeble but God is mighty and merciful. If he remembered our repented sins and was unmerciful who could survive His wrath?

This explanation of 'remembering' as action based on earlier promises is further clarified in Genesis 9, where God says that when He sees the rainbow He will remember. The rainbow is not given to us as a reminder even though it has that effect. How are we to understand this? It is not that God needs a visual stimulus to aid a failing or imperfect memory. It should be understood as a symbol of the truth that God keeps His pledges.

God acts on the basis of previous commitments made. When Jonah speaks of 'remembering the Lord' he is calling on God, in his desperate circumstances to redeem one of His troubled people. The believer may take great comfort and confidence that, 'Jesus is the same yesterday, today and forever' (Heb.13:8). He is the God who says, "For I the LORD do not change" (Malachi 3:6). People may be whimsical and moody but God is always the same. What He was in might, mercy and majesty to the saints of old He will be in might, mercy and majesty to the saints of today.

The fact that he does not change means He is immutable. This means that he is not only unchanged but also that he is unchangeable. He does not develop, learn and grow to maturity in character or knowledge because He is perfect in all His attributes. His immutability speaks of faithfulness, steadfastness, reliability, consistency and dependability. Jonah realises that although he is fickle, faithless and disobedient that he can appeal to One who is constant. He is confident that God will hear and help in his darkest hour. 'And the LORD spoke to the fish, and it vomited Jonah out upon the dry land' (2:10). It seems that wherever Jonah went he was an irritation, even the fish could not stomach him for very long! Yet it was the Lord who commanded the fish and this is further evidence of the sovereignty of God in dealing with this proud and prejudiced man.

The sovereignty of God is an important theme in the book of *Jonah*. All the way through this prophetic Old Testament book there are frequent references to the sovereignty of God. First, the Lord sent a great wind (1:4). Second, even the heathen sailors acknowledge that God has stirred up the seas according to His own pleasure (1:14). Third, the Lord provided a great fish to swallow Jonah (1:17). Fourth, Jonah attributes his being cast into the sea, not to the crew of the vessel, but to God (2:3). Fifth, he acknowledges that it was God who brought his life up from the pit (2:6). Sixth, Jonah makes the statement that "Salvation belongs to the LORD!" (2:9). Seventh, the narrative reveals that it was God who commanded the fish and Jonah was deposited on dry ground (2:10) Eighth, in chapter 4 we read that, 'the LORD God appointed a plant and made it come up over Jonah, that it might be a shade over his head, to save him from his discomfort' (4:6). Ninth, in the next verse we read, 'God appointed a worm that attacked the plant, so that it withered' (4:7). Tenth, 'God appointed a scorching east wind' (4:8).

It is not possible to read *Jonah* and doubt the sovereignty of God. There are a number of fundamental truths evident in all of this which should influence Christian belief and behaviour. It is clear that God is sovereign in the natural world. Every composition of this universe's structure and laws is under the sovereign management of God. It is not that He influences, regulates or monitors nature; He exercises His power over nature by directing and restraining its fertility and forces.

We inhabit a predominantly secular and atheistic world[21] where false religions, perverse ideologies and speculative 'philosophy' are presented as science. With a mind-boggling multiplicity of worldviews it is possible for us to forget that atheism is a falsehood and the idea that God is unconcerned or uninvolved in this world is a deception. The reality is that God is sovereign over the history of the world. In Revelation 6 John sees the bewildering chaos in the world around him. His heart is naturally fearful but God attracts his gaze upward and there he beholds an open door to heaven. God summons him to enter the throne-room where

---

[21] Though there is a growth in Islamic fundamentalism and alternative religions and new spiritualities are becoming increasingly popular.

John promptly learns that from this perspective everything has meaning and significance and all that had previously appeared to be confusing and anarchic now makes perfect sense.

The Christian is beckoned to frequently enter the throne-room of God to discover that the power of this world is not located in the White House or the Pentagon. Nor does it reside in Downing Street, or the consensus of the G8 nations, but rather in the throne-room of heaven. We are prone to neglect this truth or to forget it or disbelieve it. Every Christian needs to be aware of this truth, so let us remind one another of it especially in this generation which is bombarded with false information.

This correct, heavenly perspective of our world sustains our souls and without it one would surely become disillusioned and despairing. The grand utopia promised by the 'Enlightenment': that science and technology would eradicate power-struggles and poverty and produce a peaceful world has been utterly contradicted by two world wars, and frequent acts of major genocide. Our world is not evolving into some higher order and this theory is completely discredited by true media reporting of the depraved acts of humanity. The former Soviet Union's Marxist experiment has failed. However noble communism may have been in principle; in practice it depended on people who were corrupt and it was a system forced on societies by informants, bureaucracy and brutality.

Capitalism is also a discredited metanarrative[22] as it exploits the poor and vulnerable and allows a small few to control the vast wealth of this world. Presidents and Prime-Ministers become the puppets of their corporate benefactors. For many in this post-modern world Christianity too is a

---

[22] 'Metanarrative' means 'great story' and is a word used (negatively) by postmodernists to describe any ideology, worldview, religion or belief system. Thus Christianity, too, would be viewed as a discredited metanarrative.

discredited metanarrative and is seen as exploitative and manipulative[23] That is why it is important for Christians to stand against all injustices and detach themselves from corrupt rulers in our society.

God is sovereign in the natural world and He is also sovereign in the supernatural world. At times the manner of Christian prayer implies that we should entreat God, more fervently and frequently and hope that we have helped Him to sort things out. Perhaps some even have the opinion that if we twist God's arm hard enough or if enough of us can congregate in prayer then we can compel God by force of numbers to act as we want. These are improper approaches to prayer. We should be fully appreciative of the fact that the strength of God's supremacy and His authority does not depend on the frequency or fervency of our prayers.

Paul wrote to the Colossians because they had become subjected to heretical attack. If we have any doubts about the supremacy of Christ in all things we should remind ourselves of Paul's words to this church where he speaks of Jesus:

> He is the image of the invisible God, the firstborn of all creation. For by him all things were created, in heaven and on earth, visible and invisible, whether thrones or dominions or rulers or authorities — all things were created through him and for him. And he is before all things, and in him all things hold together. And he is the head of the body, the church. He is the beginning, the firstborn from the dead, that in everything he might be preeminent. For in him all the fullness of God was pleased to dwell, and through him to reconcile to himself all things, whether on earth or in heaven, making peace by the blood of his cross (Col.1:15-20).

---

[23] Colonial history does not show Christianity in a favourable light. Conservative evangelical resistance to civil rights issues and its participation in the oppression of others (e.g. Negroes in the Southern States of the USA) has damaged its credibility. Fundamentalist alignment with American foreign policy in Latin America and in the Middle-East has brought Christianity into disrepute.

What happened when Jesus died at Calvary? Our sins were forgiven; we were reconciled to God, rescued from hell and guaranteed a place in heaven. This is true and wonderful but that is not the complete picture as conveyed in Colossians 2. Here we read:

> And you, who were dead in your trespasses and the uncircumcision of your flesh, God made alive together with him, having forgiven us all our trespasses, by canceling the record of debt that stood against us with its legal demands. This he set aside, nailing it to the cross. He disarmed the rulers and authorities and put them to open shame, by triumphing over them in him (13-15).

Christians tend to have an egotistical regard for the cross. This egocentric view portrays salvation in terms of its advantages to believers. These benefits are certainly wonderful beyond computation. Yet, in spite of its glorious reality that is only one aspect of the bigger picture. What occurred at Calvary was of cosmic proportions. God made a public spectacle of the forces and dominions of darkness. He disarmed and defeated them. He triumphed over them and secured the victory.

Christians must not give any credibility to the counterfeit notion that God is not in sovereign control. In spite of earthquakes, tsunami, fires, floods, wars, the suffering of innocent victims, through crime and so on. It may appear that God is unaware, unconcerned and unable to do anything about suffering. This is not so.

God is sovereign in the affairs of our lives. It is a challenge to believe that He is sovereign in our particular circumstances? Will we trust God sufficiently to accept the truth that each detail of our lives is under God's direction? This great theme in the book of *Jonah* prompts us to be conscious that God is in control; that He knows all things; He is all-powerful, merciful, loving, gracious, holy and just. God sees all things and He is monarch of all He surveys. He is working out His purposes in us and through us. God deigns to use us as instruments in His grand designs but He is not ultimately dependant on us. We should not imply in the way we live, talk or pray that God needs us to help Him or He would be unable to accomplish His purposes without us. It is amazing that He condescends to employ us and engage us in His plans but our involvement in His work is not a necessary prerequisite to God accomplishing what He intends. God involves us in evangelism. He desires that we live lives that glorify Him. God desires that we speak of salvation and the things of God. He wants us to spread His Word, to preach and teach the gospel but He does not depend on us to fulfil His will. If He did I'm afraid that much of His desires would never come to fruition. God could send legions of angels to herald the glad tidings of the gospel and make stones speak of Him if He wished. Yet He has entrusted this work to His church. God is sovereign in the natural and supernatural worlds and He is supreme ruler in the particulars of our lives.

Jonah knew the doctrine of God's sovereignty, as he attributes all the circumstances of his situation to the specific intervention and control of God. Like many of us we know this in our heads, we acknowledge it to be true, we see it in Scripture, we read about it in Christian books, we sing of it in our hymns and yet it is not engraved on our hearts! So God takes us, like He took Jonah, through certain experiences, trials and traumas so that what we profess to believe is proved in the fire of trouble until we emerge triumphant. Then what we understood with our minds is branded on our souls. How often have His saints needed to be broken in order to be blessed? At his lowest point psychologically and spiritually Jonah knew it was his fault in failing to obey God that brought him to this dungeon experience. He is not trying to make excuses or pardon his mistakes. He knows that only God can absolve his rebellion and resolve his serious problem, because he understands the sovereignty of God. That is why he looks to the temple and beseeches God with the confidence of faith that he will be delivered and re-commissioned in service for God. What a merciful and mighty God we have!

Sometimes the will of God is difficult to accept, even when it is clearly stated. There are times when we have dilemmas and there is much agonising about what we ought to do. There are times that no matter what decision we take the outcome will be difficult. There are times when we know what God expects of us but it just doesn't seem to be sensible and we wonder how things could possibly work out well if we follow that course of action. Amazingly, it is possible for the Christian to think that it is better to disobey God in certain situations because it will work out better if we do! This is flawed and futile reasoning but we tend to indulge it. However, when we reject God's expressed will, things inevitably get worse.

Although Jonah's motivation and sentiment might have been commendable he was wrong to disobey God. Sometimes we sin because our motives are impure or our feelings are inappropriate. However, other times we sin even though our motives and emotions are right but it is our judgement and our will that are wrong. Jonah made a bad decision and he was determined to see it through.

The people of God can find themselves in difficult situations because of a decision of the will that they made at some point in their lives. When Jonah fled he was effectively renouncing his prophetic ministry. Many people have repudiated their faith, or a principle of their faith: the backslider, the bitter believer and the Christian who is stagnating. There are many believers who are, in a sense, at sea in their lives because of disobedience. Perhaps that is your experience. It is possible that you are a believer who feels that you once had a chance but you spurned it. But there is encouragement in *Jonah* for those who have made mistakes. Jonah was given another chance. Deliverance is possible even from what may seem to be impossible situations. We can call out to God even from the depths of despair. We can call out to God when nobody else can hear us. Surely the believer can find hope in this. Here is Jonah in the most bizarre circumstances and he cries out to God. God hears his prayer and there is a remarkable outcome; Jonah is vomited onto dry land. But what is even more astonishing is that despite all that Jonah went through he still failed to accept the will of God. He harboured a hope in his heart that God would annihilate the Ninevites.

There are many Christians who experience trouble and heartache in this world. Some are afflicted with illness and have physical pain or mental anguish or both. But it is possible to go through a great deal and learn nothing. That is disappointing if not tragic. Resisting the will of God may lead to times of trial and tribulation in the life of the believer. Perhaps we see circumstances that come into our lives as intrusions rather than divinely appointed opportunities for the transformation of our characters into the likeness of Christ. God is very active in the book of *Jonah*. God sent the storm and the fish and He is in control and orchestrating events in accordance with His sovereign will. We should not go through our Christian lives being resentful of and fighting against the providential circumstances of our mortal existence. How often it is true that our thoughts are not God's thoughts and our ways are not God's ways. We must learn to accept that His ways are infinitely better.

Jonah was in the stomach of the fish for three days and three nights. It is hard to imagine what it was like to be confined in such a place for such a period of time. It was certainly not a pleasant place to be. Whatever sense of relief he may have felt that he had not been drowned in the tempestuous sea would soon be replaced by a feeling of confinement and a sense of uncertainty about what the future may hold. Jonah was in a bad place but he survived because God was in control and he was released from his peculiar captivity.

This is interesting because metaphorically many children of God find themselves in such places. They know they have been redeemed but they are now constrained by other circumstances. Perhaps you feel that you are in a difficult work situation, a bad marriage or whatever it may be. There are some places you don't want to be; you feel trapped, you feel you are suffocating and that there is no way out. What circumstances make you feel hemmed in, helpless and hopeless?

The Lord Jesus was betrayed, deserted, denied by His closest friends, beaten, falsely tried, mocked and crucified. Jesus prayed that He might avoid drinking from that cup, yet He preferred to fulfil the divine will. Have you ever asked God to not let you drink from a certain cup?

But there is something you can do when you feel trapped. You can call out to God in prayer as Jonah did. Things were bad and Jonah started praying. You may be in a difficult place; trapped in a diseased body, struggling in a negative relationship, battling temptation or addiction, you may be experiencing financial hardship. You may feel that all your hopes, dreams, plans and ambitions are slipping away. You may feel spiritually desolate. You may feel very restricted. You may feel you have no control over your circumstances. You may be hurting. But remember Jonah thought he was in a bad place but in fact he was where God had purposefully put him. Undoubtedly it was unpleasant. Jonah prayed and God heard his prayer.

The text of the letter sent by the prophet Jeremiah (from Jerusalem to God's people living in exile in Babylon) says, "For I know the plans I have for you, declares the LORD, plans for welfare and not for evil, to give you a future and a hope" (Jer.29:11). These words must have been comforting to God's people who were in a situation, not of their own choosing but nevertheless because of their own sinfulness. God speaks tenderly to them and they know He has not forgotten them. They know He has plans which include them. These are words for us too; words that can rekindle the dying embers of hope and cause us to look to a brighter and better future.

Some places are miserable but manageable. Joseph was placed in prison. He did not deserve to be in prison but he made the best of it and soon flourished. His brothers sold him into slavery and he had endured much hardship and injustice. Yet he was later able to reassure his brothers, "you meant evil against me, but God meant it for good" (Gen.50:20). Paul was placed under house arrest and continued to be a witness for Christ at every opportunity. Moses spent forty years in the desert. That was not a confined space but nonetheless an undesirable space. These people managed. Much of our lives have to be managed. Parenting is physically tiring when children are toddlers and it is tough when they become teenagers. There are tensions and traumas and tantrums. Some jobs are difficult, the boss is awkward and the work is hard. We would prefer to be somewhere else, doing something else; anywhere else. There are times when life is barely manageable.

Paul was afflicted with a thorn in the flesh and on three occasions he pleaded with God to take it away[24]. But instead of removing it God told Paul that His grace was sufficient. So Paul managed.

The serenity prayer is not taken from the *Bible* but it is a good prayer. It says:

> God grant me the serenity
> to accept the things I cannot change;
> courage to change the things I can;
> and wisdom to know the difference.
> Living one day at a time;
> Enjoying one moment at a time;
> Accepting hardships as the pathway to peace;

---

[24] See 2 Corinthians 12.

Taking, as He did, this sinful world
as it is, not as I would have it;
Trusting that He will make all things right
if I surrender to His Will;
That I may be reasonably happy in this life
and supremely happy with Him
Forever in the next.

It is a prayer that has perspective and equilibrium.

Some space is changeable. Jonah's space changed when he got right with God. With God's help Moses and Israel left Egypt at the appointed time. When Israel became right with God they finally got out of the desert. The disciples were huddled in an upper room, afraid and in hiding. But when the Lord appeared and when the Holy Spirit fell upon them they realised they had the power to go public. God can and does sometimes dramatically intervene in the terrible spaces occupied by God's people. Think of Daniel in the lion's den and Shadrach, Meshach and Abednego in the fiery furnace and how the Lord miraculously protected and delivered them.

What is there about your life that can be changed? All things are possible to those who believe in God. You are not always trapped in unchangeable circumstances. Often in life you can make choices that bring about change. But there are other times when you have no control over the situation you find yourself in. It may be a situation of your own making. It may be a situation ordained by God. Whatever space we inhabit we should be aware that we can talk to God and know that He hears us and that He has the power to do the seemingly impossible.

William Cowper (1731-1800) experienced a great crisis in his life. When he was thirty-two years old he attempted suicide by consuming poison. When that failed he hired a horse-drawn cab to take him to the River Thames and asked to be left beside a certain bridge. He planned to take his life by jumping off that bridge into the river and drowning.

However, it was one of the foggiest nights in the city of London, and the cab got lost and couldn't find the place. Nevertheless, Cowper was determined to go through with his suicidal scheme and decided to walk to the bridge. As he groped his way through the dark night he eventually came upon his own door. He had gone in a circle and found himself back where he had begun. Determined not to concede defeat he entered his house and tried to stab himself by falling on a knife, but the blade broke. Then he tried hanging himself but after some time he was rescued by others; delirious, exhausted, but still alive! There is certainly a thin line between tragedy and comedy! Some time later when he was in better mental health, he came to understand that God's ways are mysterious and wonderful. He penned a hymn that encapsulates the awe he had come to own regarding God's sovereign ways:

God moves in a mysterious way

His wonders to perform;
He plants His footsteps in the sea
And rides upon the storm.

Deep in unfathomable mines
Of never-failing skill
He treasures us His bright designs
And works His sovereign will.

Ye fearful saints, fresh courage take;
The clouds ye so much dread
Are big with mercy and shall break
In blessings on your head.

Judge not the Lord by feeble sense.
But trust Him for His grace;
Behind a frowning providence
He hides a smiling face.

His purposes will ripen fast,
Unfolding every hour;
The bud may have a bitter taste,
But sweet will be the flower.

> Blind unbelief is sure to err
> And scan His work in vain;
> God is His own Interpreter,
> And He will make it plain.[25]

When the Christian faces trying times he can trust God who is at work for the good of His children and the glory of His name.

Jonah is centre stage in the first two chapters of the book, with God in the background working out His grand designs. However in the latter two chapters the emphasis shifts from Jonah to God. This is where the text has been leading all along. In some way this is like the Christian experience, especially at times of suffering. Our trials and tribulations should bring us on a journey from self-centredness to God-consciousness.

---

[25] It is unlikely that Cowper could have written this hymn without having first gone through the ordeal outlined above. It is truly marvellous that, 'All things work together for the good of those who love God…' (Rom.8:28).

6.

Grace for the Guilty

However, in spite of all that we have said about the sovereignty of God it should be noted that, although it is a glorious doctrine, it is in fact a sub-theme of this Old Testament book. The central theme of *Jonah* is indisputably the graciousness of God's heart.

It is our privilege and delight to approach Scripture with eagerness and expectation to hear what the Lord has to say. We are all familiar with the story of *Jonah* and perhaps feel there is nothing more to see in this book or that we understand the lessons it teaches. In spite of such un-teachable attitudes the Holy Spirit can shed fresh light on the most familiar passages of God's Word. God will not add new truth to His Word but he can illuminate and elucidate truth that is revealed in a manner previously concealed. What a delight it is when God opens our eyes, ears, hearts and minds in this way. We are not in pursuit of novelty but God is able to take a text that appears sterile and educate, instruct and edify even weary and sceptical souls.

God is omniscient, and knowing all things means that He knows all about us, our personal circumstances; emotional, psychological, spiritual, financial and filial; all that can be known. He knows where we are in our pilgrimage, our devotional lives, our fellowship with other believers, our service and ministries. The Holy Spirit delights to whisper His Word into each heart that is attentive for

His voice. When God speaks to us we know it beyond doubt and it is both humbling and surprising. Even though we desired to hear we feel special in the sense that God has put His hand upon us and drawn us aside to whisper a personal word of comfort, exhortation or rebuke. As we read the book of *Jonah* may the Holy Spirit speak to us through the familiar and dramatic narrative!

If the opening words of the third chapter of *Jonah* sound familiar that is because they are very similar to the opening words of chapter 1. In 1:1 we read, 'Now the word of the LORD came to Jonah'. However, in 3:1 we read, 'Then the word of the LORD came to Jonah the second time'. Jonah's response is different on this occasion. So we read, 'Jonah arose and went to Nineveh, according to the word of the LORD' (3:3). The great theme of *Jonah* is God's character, which is slow to anger and abounding in love. God is merciful and gracious even (perhaps especially) to His rebellious servants. The fact that God is 'slow to chide and swift to bless' is presented to us in the fact that God allows Jonah a second chance. Undoubtedly he had failed God and flagrantly rebelled against the clearly expressed command of the Lord. He had violated his privileged position as a prophet of God. God had every right to be angry and to punish Jonah. But God reveals to us something essential about His nature in the way he deals with Jonah. His merciful, gracious and loving attributes come to the fore and He affords Jonah another opportunity to fulfil the commission. Thus God reveals to us that He is the God of second chances! He did not abandon this pitiful man. He did not say you have had your chance and you blew it, and now I have no further use for you. He did not revoke his ministry. He did not withdraw his mission. In fact he did not even rebuke Jonah for his rebellious and wayward behaviour!

We should not gloss over this. God does not deal with us as our sins deserve, for if He did who could stand righteous before him? God did not reject this man who had disgraced himself before the crew of the ship. Jonah was running away from God, rejecting his mission and setting out to start a new life free from service for God. Here is a missionary in trouble but God treats him sympathetically. He has had great trauma in his life and failed his master. Many missionary societies today might treat such an employee very differently. Would his resignation be requested or would he be summarily dismissed for gross misconduct and airbrushed out of existence? How sad it is that we lack the compassion and benevolence of God when dealing with people who let us down. We brand them as failures, revoke their contracts and send them back to the world shamed, disgraced and humiliated. We feel justified in treating the disobedient trouble maker in this way because after all we have rules and regulations and policies and procedures to observe. A serious breach of expectations and obligations of this nature, we say, warrants proportional action. Aren't you glad God does not take out the divine policy manual of Scripture when you fail? Aren't you relieved that He does not cite policy and procedure in chapter and verse? He does not come with ungracious and undignified haste to punish us when we let Him down. If He kept a record of our wrongdoing we would be condemned.

The essential theme of this chapter is God's clemency. Every word is structured around it. God is emphasising that He is one who offers second chances to His people. In spite of the fact that Jonah was so obstinate and persistent in rebellion and disobedience to God he has survived his ordeal only because God intervened to save him. Jonah is re-commissioned by God to the original job assigned to him. 'God's gifts and his calling are irrevocable' (Rom.11:29).

This is the excellent manner of God's methods. He offers grace to the guilty, mercy to those who have no merit, light to the lost, relationship to the rejected and a hand up to those who stumbled into the pit of despair. With God there is always a way forward, though every door seems shut He will not fail for He will extend His hand in help to the helpless and bring hope to the hopeless and love to those who do not deserve it.

The way God dealt with Jonah and other saints of old is the way He deals with His people in every generation. The *Bible* records, for our benefit, some of the second chances that have been given to people. David, the great king of Israel, an outstanding leader of God's people, a champion warrior who slew the heavily armed and experienced Philistine warrior Goliath, a giant, with only a sling and stone. These were the weapons of a shepherd boy for frightening away animals that would prey on the flock of sheep he was tending in the fields. But they were wielded in faith. God favoured him and he was anointed king by God's servant. Yet he sinned so terribly. He committed adultery with Bathsheba, which was conceived in lust at an idle moment when he should have been leading his troops in battle. He commissioned the murder of this woman's husband, Uriah, who is listed as one of David's bravest soldiers. He had committed grievous wrongs and deserved to incur the wrath of God. His actions brought disaster upon himself, upon his family, upon the nation and upon the reputation of God. All was in ruins, but God restored him! God gave him a second chance. When we read that great penitential prayer of David (Psalm 51) and bear in mind the background that gives rise to this plea for mercy we hear the words of a broken spirit, whose only hope is mercy. It is to God's mercy that David appeals and he does not find God lacking to supply such mercy. God refers to David as a man after His own heart. David was restored after he was confronted by Naman, the prophet. He repented about a year after the adulterous affair and the latter period of his monarchy was better than the earlier years of his reign.

Abraham is described as 'a friend of God' and yet we read in Scripture how he lied about Sarah and said she was his sister when she was his wife; an untruth that could have had disastrous consequences. Consider Jacob, a liar and a cheat whose life is full of trouble he incurred because of his behaviour. He deceived his father, cheated his brother, battled and bargained with God Himself. But God broke him in order to bless him and he was changed in name and nature. Israel was his new title. The mercy of God is beautiful to contemplate and it is beautiful to imitate such a divine quality. But all this begs the question, why don't we see more of it in Christian circles?

When we consider Simon Peter we see a man who was passionate, though perhaps impulsive and volatile. He was one of the Lord's closest disciples, an apostle of Jesus. Yet he dramatically and repeatedly denied the Lord Jesus. Nevertheless, within six weeks he is restored, not just to fellowship but to renewed and increased responsibility in service within the kingdom of God! We might tend to take the opposite action against someone who lied repeatedly and denied his master. Left to our meagre mercy he would be demoted or dismissed. On the day of Christ's resurrection 'Mary Magdalene, Mary the mother of James and Salome bought spices so that they might go to anoint Jesus' body' (Mk.16:1). When they entered the tomb and realised that Christ had risen they were instructed to, 'go tell his disciples, and Peter…' (Mk.16:7). That phrase 'and Peter' is truly remarkable. He is mentioned by name. Surely the intention is to reassure him that he belongs to that close band of brothers in Christ. It must have brought great comfort to the apostle who was probably feeling so remorseful and ashamed of his deeds and words. But that is the kind of compassionate God we have. He cares for the individual and especially those in most need of His mercy.

Peter had denied Jesus three times. In chapter 21 of John's gospel Jesus displays His resurrected power in the miraculous catch of 153 large fish and He invites His disciples to eat the meal of bread and fish which He had prepared on burning coals. What follows is commonly known as the 'Reinstatement of Peter'. Jesus asks Peter three time to profess his love for Him. On each occasion after Peter expressed his love Jesus instructed him, 'feed my lambs', 'take care of my sheep' and 'feed my sheep'. These are not casual or sentimental words of consolation from Christ but words of re-commissioning and delegation of significant responsibility.

Have you ever been curious about how the other disciples felt about this conversation as they sat together after their breakfast around the fire on the shore of the Sea of Tiberius? Perhaps they thought that Jesus was taking a serious risk. If we were witnesses to this conversation we too might have felt that at such a vital and decisive time in the history of the early church Jesus was giving responsibility to a man who was prone to impulsive behaviour, aggression (he had sliced off the right ear of Malchus, the servant of the High Priest) and cowardice. Perhaps we would have marvelled at Christ's behaviour. Maybe we would even have thought that Jesus is a poor judge of character. Would we entrust responsibility to a man who had failed? Maybe the other disciples felt that one of them should have been chosen because of their more favourable temperament and consistent behaviour.

Jonah had run away from God in deliberate disobedience. Although he attempted to sever his relationship with God the Lord did not wash His hands of him. God does not quickly dismiss Jonah. He has no intention of finding a replacement to fulfil that mission. Rather he pursues Jonah. God has gone to extraordinary lengths to ensure that Jonah is restored to right relationship and He puts Jonah back on course right at the very point of his departure from God's will. God delivered Jonah from a ghastly death. He restored him physically and spiritually and then recalled and re-commissioned him. That is ample evidence of the gracious heart of God. 'The word of the LORD came to Jonah a second time'. No condemnation or remonstrating, just re-commissioning.

The word of the Lord may also come again to men who have *not* failed God or fled from him. It might come again to men whom God has allowed to go through difficult circumstances. Job was such a man. His difficulties were not related to non-compliance, insubordination or defiance of God's commands. On the contrary it was because of his faithfulness to God that he went through many trials and suffered terrible loss, anguish and distress.

We can also cite the story of Joseph and how he encountered great difficulty because of his faithfulness. He was not adulterous, disloyal or untrustworthy. Yet he was imprisoned on false charges. It was because of his integrity that he found himself in trouble. He fled from an occasion to sin. We are naïve if we fail to realise that obedience to God may lead to difficult circumstances.

The illustration of the potter and the clay in chapter 18 of Jeremiah is a beautiful picture of how God works with His people. Jeremiah sees the potter at the wheel in his workshop but the vessel he was fashioning was marred. So the potter reshapes the disfigured clay into an unblemished vessel. That is what the potter does with misshapen clay that does not meet the expectations He has. This is a picture of God, who takes what is spoiled, blemished and flawed and perfects it according to His matchless craftsmanship into what His mind deems suitable, so that we are fit for purpose. The divine potter takes us, delicate and often misshapen pieces of clay in His hands and He reshapes us. We are a work in progress in the hands of the Master. God does not reject us as useless when we fail but He refashions us and strengthens us in the intense heat of the kiln. At the outset we are shapeless lumps of clay but when His work is complete we will be unblemished and intact vessels fit for use in His kingdom. We are not consigned to the reject bin because of our flaws and neither are we labelled 'seconds' and valued accordingly.

God is patient and longsuffering and His Word contains many metaphors and similes which stress the second chances and the grace God grants to His people. Perhaps you are conscious of your failings and aware that you have botched the work that He has given you to do. Maybe you have been unsuccessful in some spiritual project and you feel you have disappointed God and let others down. Maybe you have decided that you don't come up to scratch and that you will never make the grade. Your feel that your failures are obvious to everybody and think you have had your chance and blew it. Your transgression is transparent and it has been blatantly manifested to all. You have no expectation of a second chance and so you may write yourself off as inadequate, ineffective, unworthy and unwanted. Maybe you feel that God could never use you again.

You might be like Peter on that morning after the night of his denials of Jesus. Your heart is broken and all that you hoped for has disappeared. It's all over you tell yourself and now you have to go back to fishing because you know you are good at that and you have to earn a living. I can only imagine what was going through Peter's mind in his grief and guilt but I know that many others since Peter have failed and believed they are spiritually bankrupt and have nothing to contribute to the Lord's work. In the eyes of others we may be unsuccessful and even untrustworthy, but in the eyes of God disfigured clay is the raw material for his designs.

Don't let that delicate flickering flame of hope be quenched by the unmerciful and ungracious attitudes of some of God's people. Cradle it close to your heart and let the Holy Spirit softly fan it into a flame that will burn brightly and light the path God wants you to take. The

Word of the Lord will come to you a second time or a third or fourth time. God never gives up on His people and He will not discard you like some worthless piece of broken machinery. He is merciful and this is evident in *Jonah* and right throughout Scripture. Jesus said, "Blessed are the merciful, for they shall receive mercy" (Mt.5:7). It is a cold world outside the narrow sphere of Christian mercy, an inhospitable and desolate habitat where abandoned and friendless 'failures' slowly fade away.

In the parable of the 'Prodigal Son' we encounter the recalcitrant young man returning home. We are not told how long he has been away but it appears that every day since his departure his father spent some time looking into the distant horizon, longing to see his son reappear, his old eyes growing dim with age. But his heart yearns and hopes that one day his son will return. Then one day he sees a figure in the distance and though it is blurred and indistinct he dares to hope and his heartbeat quickens at the prospect of what might be. Perhaps this has happened on other occasions only to end in disappointment as some stranger treks his way along another path. But now as the figure draws nearer this venerable man hoists the hem of his garment and races swiftly to meet his son. Perhaps the young prodigal is stinking of the swine he tended in the final days of his rebellion. His father does not care that he has come from a pigsty. He spontaneously expresses his great love for his son in a crushing embrace and with kisses and tears. The father does not interrogate or scold his son or reprimand him for his foolishness. He does not hold him at a distance or reserve his affection until the son proves himself worthy of reinstatement as a member of the family. The father waits and wants his son to come back and take his place at the family table. He does not speak angrily to him. It is a story of a forgiving father and it challenges us to look within ourselves and ask if we as sons of God have His merciful disposition.

Maybe the Word of the Lord is coming right now to you, a second time. Maybe you can remember a time, in your Christian life, when there was an explicit act of defiance or non-compliance with God's instructions. Or perhaps God has allowed you to go through turbulent times that have nothing to do with an act of waywardness. Are you in troubled waters? Are you insubordinate like Jonah or innocent like Joseph and Job?

The Lord never quits. If you have messed up, then, like Jonah you can ask forgiveness. One of the absent constituents in Christian attitude and action is the essentials and rudimentary element of mercy and grace. Sadly, it is often those who believe their theology is the most perfect who reveal less of the grace of God. However correct your theology may be it is impotent unless it reflects the mercy and grace of God. Those who are prone to reject people who fail are poor ambassadors for Christ. We are careful to guard the reputations of our churches and missions and this is correct. But when we do that by treating those who fail as expendable and exclude them we must realise that the reputation of our church or mission in heaven has been greatly sullied. How little we understand and practice the grace and mercy of God. We cannot fully comprehend the scope of such divine attributes of love.

Manifesting mercy is of profound pastoral value. Many Christians carry burdens of guilt that they should have divested themselves of at Calvary. God has dealt with the sin, but sometimes we cannot forgive ourselves and the guilt lingers on and torments us. All of us are less willing to forgive than God! Even when God is embracing us we struggle with Him. The Word of the Lord will always come to us a second time, He does not give us just one chance, even an irritable schoolteacher can do better than that!

However, knowing that the Word of the Lord will come to us a second time must not make us impudent or smug. We must not take the attitude that if we refuse to comply now He will reinstate us at some other time when it is more convenient and congenial to our minds. This would be presumptuous and arrogant. It is wrong to take for granted that if we refuse to do as we are told now that there will automatically be another opportunity at some later stage to comply with God's instructions. There is a danger that we would take the grace of God for granted.

The third chapter of *Jonah* is focused on a second chance not only for Jonah but also for Nineveh. We have already identified some things about Nineveh (such as its *greatness*). The assignment allocated to Jonah was a momentous mission. The text repeats several times that Nineveh is a 'great city' [1:2; 3:1, 3; 4:11]. It is frequently described as 'great' so that we understand this place to be a well populated, influential and strategic city. It is not a small or insignificant place. It is great in size and significance. It was built by Noah's great-grandson, Nimrod. Jonah's mission was to reveal the God of Israel as the universal God. Thus God reveals something new in the book of *Jonah* as He is portrayed as a God whose mercy and grace extends beyond the borders of Israel, to all nations and even (perhaps one might even say *especially*) to the iniquitous, like the Assyrians.

When we think about the mission given to Jonah (1:2) it must have appeared not only dangerous but peculiar. Nineveh was one of the principal cities or perhaps the cruellest regime on earth in the eighth century B.C. Jonah is commanded (not requested or invited) by God to preach against Nineveh's great evil. God was doing something new in sending Jonah with a message to this heathen habitation and that must have seemed strange to Jonah. We are not unlike Jonah in this regard, as we are slow to hear, understand and obey anything that is not processed and passed by our own intellectual faculties and expectations about how things should be. Tradition takes on a sanctity of its own and the thought of doing something different is rejected on the basis that 'we have never done things like this before'. We should be custodians of good traditions but beware of becoming prisoners of tradition *per se*. The captains of conservatism are often merely captives of the conventional.

God can and does act in ways that at times seem peculiar to us. We tend to form habits; ways of doing things and ways of thinking that become immutable laws. Eventually we see any deviation in thinking or digression in ways of doing things as wrong, or at least as an unprecedented and unwarranted departure from tried and trusted traditions! We have no biblical warrant for many of our traditions and assumptions but would tend to see any breach in structure or procedure as errant, if not evil. So before we judge Jonah let us ask ourselves if we would be willing to obey God if the command seemed bizarre to our minds. We might rather think of such a thing as a psychotic episode where we had some kind of auditory hallucination. We, or others, might dismiss it as an absurd departure from God's ways. But that is probably what Jonah thought; God does not send His prophets to those outside the household of Israel. God's grace and mercy do not rightly belong to these enemies of the Almighty and if God forgives these, our enemies, we will eventually be subjugated by them and absorbed into their culture. Then we will no longer be a distinctive people, favoured by God to be the custodians of truth, inheritors of grace and beneficiaries of merciful blessings. Israel had come to expect God to deal favourably and exclusively with them. They had forgotten or never clearly understood that they were to become the source of blessing to all nations. They were the privileged first recipients of grace and mercy ultimately intended for people of all tribes and nations.

So the great wickedness of Nineveh forms a perfect backdrop which allows the mercy and grace of God to be displayed in all its magnificence. The depth of Nineveh's depravity highlights the magnitude and immensity of God's mercy and grace.

Why should God be concerned with Nineveh, this great symbol of human evil? Why does God not simply destroy these vicious people, who were renowned for their savagery and barbaric practices? God has gone to great lengths to get his rebellious servant into Nineveh to preach. Why bother bringing a prophet from a distant land (perhaps 600 miles away) to do this?

The book of *Jonah* and its message enables us to look into the heart of God. There we see that God loves all His creatures, irrespective of race, colour, religion or their state of righteousness! Do you believe it? Even the worst heretic and the vilest sinner are loved by God. Yes, God loathes and detests the wicked things they teach and do but He loves all people everywhere. In stark contrast to the vast love of God and the immensity of His mercy we see the shrivelled and small heart of Jonah, God's servant. The problem is not just Jonah because he was typical of God's people at that time. He is not exceptional in his attitude. He is typical in his contempt for the idea that God could extend His affections to such heathen reprobates. Jonah's love is small and constricted but God's love is immense and immeasurable. How do we measure up? Are we forgiving, gracious and merciful like God (as we ought to be) or are we like Jonah? What limits are there to our forgiveness? Why do we reserve grace as if it was a rare commodity that needs to be rationed? Why is the world often more merciful than the church? If we are not demonstrating the benevolence of God then we are misrepresenting Him. If we think His boundless forgiveness, ample grace and munificent mercy is restricted to certain peoples and inappropriate to others then we misunderstand God and not only do we misrepresent Him but we are idolaters because we worship an image of God that is entirely false.

Just as God did not abandon Jonah He does not forsake

the Ninevites in their great need. God is a God of justice and holiness and He does not tolerate sin in any form. Nevertheless He takes no delight in the destruction of the iniquitous inhabitants of Nineveh. There's wideness in God's mercy that we cannot comprehend. We all have our own limits to forgiveness, grace and mercy; sins that feature on our unforgivable list.

We tend to give the impression that the church is a place for those who have repented and forsaken all their sins. I would like to find a church where there is no pride, jealousy, prejudice, pettiness, envy or strife. But those concealed sins, the things that happen behind closed doors and in secret, those wrong attitudes are smuggled into the church all the time.

But God's mercy is not infinite. A lot of people in our contemporary society find the notion of a God of judgement to be problematic in their faith system and private beliefs. Over the past decade (or perhaps longer) it is noticeable when attending funerals that the deceased are 'always' deemed to be in 'heaven'. A funeral is not the best place to preach about hell and judgement because those who are grieving need comfort. But it is a different matter to suggest or even state categorically that a person is 'in heaven' when that person never gave any indication of repentance or faith in Christ. The biggest blackguards on the planet are eulogised and scoundrels are presented as saints.

The idea of a God who is punitive is objectionable to many but Scripture clearly presents God's attributes, and justice, holiness and wrath are some of His characteristics. Obviously the declaration that all the dead go to heaven is no more than a peculiar way of expressing compassion for the bereaved in what is probably a genuine attempt to bring comfort and solace to those who are grieving. It may not be the official teaching of his church and by now it has become no more than a pious platitude because the drunken wife-beater and the dear old lady who attended church regularly are likewise pronounced to be in heaven. I'm not suggesting that pastors and ministers of Christ's church make judgements about the eternal destiny of souls. But there are funerals where we are celebrating the lives of believers who have gone to be with the Lord. There are others we may not be sure about and there are some who have shown no evidence of spiritual regeneration. It is right to handle all of these situations sensitively, to pastor the bereaved and comfort those who sorrow for the passing of the life of a loved one. However, to have a blanket policy of declaring the dead to be in heaven is unbiblical and merely offers false hope to some and no hope at all to those who realise that this is merely what the minister always says anyway.

The greatness of Nineveh's wickedness emphasises the grandeur of God's grace. Sadly God's merciful nature sometimes contrasts with the meanness of men's minds. This is summed up in the hymn by Michael Baughen:

There's a wideness in God's mercy

Like the wideness of the sea;
There's a kindness in His justice
Which is more than liberty.

There is plentiful redemption
In the blood that has been shed;
There is joy for all the members
in the sorrows of the Head.

There is grace enough for thousands
Of new worlds as great as this;
There is room for fresh creations
In that upper home of bliss.

For the love of God is broader
Than the measures of man's mind;
And the heart of the Eternal
Is most wonderfully kind.

But we make His love too narrow
By false limits of our own;
And we magnify His strictness
With a zeal He will not own.

If our love were but more simple
We should take Him at His word;
And our lives would be illumined
By the presence of the Lord.

Although this hymn emphasises the vastness of God's mercy I think it is interesting to note that the author compares this to the wideness of the sea. It should be pointed out that however wide the ocean may be there is in fact a shoreline. There are limits to the breadth of the seas and there are limits to God's mercy; alluded to in perhaps too subtle a manner in the above hymn. The notion that God's mercy is *infinite* is theologically wrong.

7.

<u>Potent Preaching</u>

There are some Christian churches who like to major on God's holiness, wrath and justice. It is the keynote of many sermons. To disproportionately present some attributes of God's character while neglecting to give due proportion to other characteristics of God is to present a caricature of God. There are some churches today who feel the love, grace, mercy and kindness of God is overemphasised by certain sections of the Christian community and so they seek to redress this in their churches by addressing what they believe to be neglected biblical teaching.

This reminds me of the fact that in Ireland newspapers have traditional political connections. To read the *Irish Press*[26] was to be presented with the politics of republicanism and anti-treaty sentiment and the aspiration for a 32 county Ireland. If this was the only newspaper available to us then we would not have a free and impartial press. However, there are other newspapers with opposite views, such as the *Irish Independent* and the *Irish Times*. What makes Ireland a country with a free press is not the absence of prejudice but the balance of coverage found in different newspapers. I sometimes think of the Christian church like this. It is the balance of different biases rather than any monopoly on 'truth' that really presents a truer picture of God rather than any one group, especially the group that dots every 'i' and crosses every 't', where the interrogative is disdained in favour of the doctrinaire.

---

[26] No longer in existence

The more intimate one becomes with God the more one comes to know Him; not as a God of anger, wrath and judgement but rather as a God of mercy, grace, love and kindness. I cannot deny His wrath, judgement and anger but I have seen the face of the one who lifted me out of the pit of despair and I have seen grace, love, mercy and kindness in those eyes and in every wrinkle and fold of that divine face I have seen anguish for the lost, love for the saved, forgiveness and friendship for failures. He has been my companion in times of doubt and depression. He has been my helper in times of trouble. He has been my physician in times of illness and pain. He has put gifts in my hands and mouth; hands that have failed Him and a tongue that has failed Him. Yet he has not taken back these gifts.

The portraits of Jesus I see in the gospels are of one who is tender, compassionate, kind, gracious and merciful. In my relationship with Him I have found Him to be strong when I am weak, to guide the way when I am lost or confused, to listen when I complain and to answer gently. He supplies courage when I am fearful and when all the doors to the future seem closed and I find myself in the dungeon of despair again He brings light and whispers that in a little while one of these doors will open. As a recipient of His saving and sustaining grace and as a beneficiary of His mercy in my Christian life the only true testimony I can give of God is this: He is a God of 'love, joy, peace, patience, kindness, goodness, faithfulness, gentleness and self-control.' He has been all this to me and more than that He has been a friend. This is the God I know and love and it is in Him I glory and it is of Him I will speak. He is my dignity, my peace, my guide, my companion, my redeemer and friend.

In order to wholly understand and value the mercy and grace of God in its unfathomable depth and immeasurable dimensions we must first understand the depth of our own depravity and God's prerogative to exercise anger and judgement. The mercy of God is best understood by those who know they have no merit of their own and no defence in His court accept to appeal for mercy. When we consider God's entitlement to judge and His right to anger then we can see His mercy in perspective and that is the beginning of knowing anything of the love of God.

When the prophet enters Nineveh he starts to proclaim this exceedingly short but overwhelmingly strong message.[27] Although chapter 2 of Jonah is the prophet's prayer to God from within the belly of the fish, I am inclined to think that it is possibly also part of his preaching in Nineveh. It reads remarkably like a personal testimony and would fit in with his message calling for repentance to such an almighty God. I confess it is nothing more than a speculation but one day we might have opportunity to ask him about that sermon! Some Christians misunderstand the true nature of God by supposing that His initial impulse toward sinners is to condemn and punish. But God's primary instinct is to forgive and even to forget the wrongdoing of those who repent.

Here is the man Jonah, in hostile territory, proclaiming the Word of the Lord to a violent people. There is a tremendous response to the preaching. Familiarity with the events recorded in the book of *Jonah* may diminish our sense of astonishment at such a significant outcome to the preaching of Jonah, "Yet forty days, and Nineveh shall be overthrown!" (3:4) and the response is recorded, 'the people of Nineveh believed God. They called for a fast and put on sackcloth'.

We read that, 'The word reached the king of Nineveh, and he arose from his throne, removed his robe, covered himself with sackcloth, and sat in ashes' (3:6). The king even

---

[27] Possibly a summary statement of his key theme in preaching the need for repentance in the light of impending judgement.

issued a decree that all people and animals were to be covered in sackcloth and not to eat or drink anything. But it seems from the sequence of events in the narrative account that the people had already responded by declaring a fast and putting on sackcloth and ashes.

We are told, 'the people of Nineveh believed God'. This shows that the Ninevites' repentance was a genuine response to the Word of God and not merely obedience to their king's proclamation. The king exhorted his people in this proclamation 'let every one turn from his evil way and from the violence that is in his hands' (3:8). He acknowledges their wickedness and especially identifies their violence as something that must be set aside. When the word of the Lord came to Jonah a second time God told him, "Arise, go to Nineveh, that great city, and preach to it the message that I tell you" (3:2). We are then told, 'Jonah arose and went to Nineveh, according to the word of the LORD' (3:3).

We must assume that Jonah faithfully proclaimed the word the Lord had given him, "Yet forty days, and Nineveh shall be overthrown!" (3:4). That would make a rather short and repetitive sermon and does not adequately explain the king's hope that God would be merciful and compassionate. Neither does it show anything of God's desire that they should avail of the grace available to them in repentance. This would seriously misrepresent God's true character. The king obviously did not interpret what Jonah said as the announcement of an inexorable cataclysmic event that would occur after a period of forty days. He had some reason to hope that God might relent and turn from His fierce anger and that they might not be destroyed. He also demonstrated some knowledge of the customary Hebrew practice of wearing sackcloth and ashes as a symbol of genuine repentance.

The people also appear to have this knowledge prior to the king's edict being proclaimed. The only plausible explanation for this is that what is recorded of Jonah's preaching is a summary statement of his key theme in preaching the need for repentance in the light of impending judgement. It is therefore likely that his message was more comprehensive than the mere pronouncement of judgement and that it included a call to repentance and some instruction on how to demonstrate that repentance. It is likely that he told his own story (his testimony/prayer of chapter 2) which included the statements: "Those who regard worthless idols forsake their own mercy" (2:8). In other words they forfeit the grace that could be theirs and because of their regard for vain idols they forsake the steadfast love which God is willing to bestow upon them. Jonah proclaims, "Salvation belongs to the LORD!" (2:9).

If we take the recorded proclamation as all that the prophet said, then he preached only impending judgement. If we examine the text it does not record any invitation to repent or instructions about how one should demonstrate repentance. This reinforces the view that his prayer in chapter 2 also constituted part of his preaching message. In that passage, Jonah attributes his redemption to God, where, he confesses that God brought his life up out of the pit. But the verse already quoted above: "Those who regard worthless idols forsake their own mercy" appears to be something that was said to others. Also the statement in verse 9 already cited: "Salvation belongs to the LORD!" fits in well with expounding the message of repentance.

How natural it would have been for Jonah to tell of his experience and I am rather inclined to think that his appearance, after three days confinement in the stomach of the fish suggests that he probably had to give some account for his peculiar appearance. He had, after all, been effectively marinated in the gastric juices of this creature and this would surely have had some obvious effect on how he looked.

It must be noted also that Scripture says, 'The Ninevites believed God'. The text does not say the Ninevites believed Jonah! Jonah was a conduit for the message of God and the fact that the text tells us that the people believed God demonstrates that they had no doubt about the prophets credibility as God's spokesperson. When a man is called and commissioned by God and given a certain work to do then God will bless that work. The power of the Word of God to save lives is extraordinary but it should not be astonishing to those who profess to believe that it is His Word. It is important to note that the people believed God. They did not think Jonah was making this up. They did not think that it was the message of a man but recognised it as a message from God. Credit must be given to Jonah for not interfering with the message so that it remained a pure and potent proclamation from God. Many 'preachers' today are prone to tell little stories and anecdotes[28] and not engage in expository preaching, probably because they have lost confidence in the power of Scripture to prevail in the hearts of men.

From the greatest to the least (perhaps a reference to relative age or status) the people of Nineveh confess their sin, believe God, declare a fast and clothe themselves in sackcloth and ashes to signify repentance. In this generation many Christians seem to have lost confidence in the power of the Word of God. But the preaching of the Word of God in this Old Testament book is a reminder to us that the Scripture can penetrate the most unlikely hearts and minds if it is faithfully preached. The Word of God is a living, dynamic power that arouses faith and stimulates obedience in its hearers. The age in which we live is a period of diminished confidence in the preached Word. But evangelistic preaching is one of God's ordained and primary means of bringing conviction of sin and conversion to sinners. Preaching can inspire believers to accept the

---

[28] There is nothing wrong with using illustrations sparingly to shed light on some truth; in fact it can be quite refreshing. What I am objecting to here is the overindulgence of this at the expense of expository preaching.

commissioning of God for service in pastoral ministry or missionary endeavour. The Word of God can accomplish more than we expect or even dare to imagine possible. This generation needs renewed faith in the power of God's Word.

Jonah was commanded by God to go to Nineveh and proclaim a message from God. We should note that he was not asked to go if given the opportunity at some time when it was convenient for him. God did not say, "Jonah, if you are ever in that region I would be obliged if you could do something for Me." God did not say: "go and find a place to live in Nineveh and invite people to dine with you. Have special parties and topical talks and build friendships. Then at some opportune moment you can mention Me and their need for a relationship with God." There is a regal note of authority in this commission to Jonah. He is commanded, not requested. Likewise the 'Great Commission' which Jesus gave to His disciples strikes a note of authority: "All authority has been given to Me in heaven and on earth. Go therefore and make disciples of all the nations…" (Mt.28:18-19).

Today we are fond of building bridges and we have forgotten the need to burn bridges. The contemporary approach is to allay people's misgivings and mistrust by having events that show us as ordinary people, no different to themselves. We entertain and amuse them and divert their attention from the grave reality of their sinful condition. We say we must not confront them with the truth as that will frighten them off. So we become careful about what we say and avoid explicit biblical content and focus on making our guests feel good. We try to be as inoffensive as possible for fear of losing their interest. This is pathetic oration not worthy of the word 'preaching' and certainly nothing like the kind of prophetic preaching that is needed today.

It is interesting to observe that there's nothing powerful about Jonah. In fact he was a very reluctant preacher and in some ways he is a ridiculous character. Have you ever wondered why God did not merely appoint somebody else to do the job? Surely there was somebody else on the panel of potential candidates who would be more willing to cooperate! The disparity in the size, significance and splendour of Nineveh compared with the feeble and unenthusiastic spectacle of the preacher, provides a dramatic contrast.

Imagine what Jonah must have looked like after he wriggles free from the pool of fish vomit on the beach. He would have been a very strange sight. Just imagine Jonah in such a messy state entering Nineveh, a prosperous and sophisticated city. He must have looked conspicuous. I imagine this unkempt and dishevelled man shuffling his way through crowded streets and people staring at his scruffy and bedraggled appearance. I imagine that he smelled of fish and attracted quite a bit of curiosity. Perhaps he attracted some notice as a target of derision. Yet God took this wayward, unappealing, unsightly, smelly and even repellent individual and made him the most successful evangelist in Old Testament history! It's not his gift of oratory or powers of persuasion. If we are to take the proclamation recorded as the entire message preached by Jonah then it constitutes one of the shortest sermons ever delivered, by one of the strangest people who ever lived! If this was his complete sermon we should note that it did not have three alliterative points! In fact it has not much more than three words! The words he preached, as conveyed in the text add up to a total of eight words![29] Whatever he said, we know that it was a message God had given to him, which resulted in repentance.

God defies our expectations by taking the foolish things of this world to confound the wise and lead the way to salvation. There are no better methods than God's methods

---

[29] In the N.K.J.V. other versions may have a slightly different word.

and we have nothing to teach Him about evangelism. I believe in the simplicity and superiority of preaching. Many other means of evangelism are effective but we must never allow them to displace the simplicity of preaching. Even the most peculiar of men, failures in the eyes of everybody can be triumphant in service for Christ. By trying to be clever we merely lessen the effect of the gospel. It is easy to win arguments and even convince people of the credibility of the Christian message but conviction of sin and conversion to Christ is uniquely the work of the Holy Spirit. No man can win souls for Jesus but he can faithfully proclaim the Word of God and trust the outcome to the Holy Spirit.

Jonah is like the street preacher, an object of ridicule and scorn, contempt or indifference. We might say that the era of street preaching is past and even that preaching is inappropriate in an age where oratory is no longer respected as it used to be. We might argue for a more visual or dramatic presentation of the gospel message but this is wrong. It is wrong because God revealed Himself in words; He is a God who speaks. The visual representation was always forbidden in Scripture because it led to false ideas of God and idolatry. God communicates through words, an intelligible, simple and serious message. One might argue that God also revealed Himself in Christ, but Jesus was not merely a visual aid. God the Son chose to preach and teach and we have, not four gospels but four complimentary accounts of one gospel, in written form.

Here in *Jonah* we have a lovely depiction of the mercy of God as he engages this insubordinate servant and makes him an instrument to accomplish His good purposes for the people of Nineveh. He does this by giving Jonah a message to proclaim. In spite of Jonah's failure, frailty and flawed character the Lord still used him. We write people off, brand them as failures unfit for service but in contrast God says He prefers to use the man who has been marred but remade. God still prefers to use the man who has, metaphorically, been in the belly of the fish. Whereas we see the person who has been broken as useless God sees such a person as useful. We find God reversing our values, principles and expectations.

Have you ever seen a portrait where the true character of the person is represented in the image? Well the last verse of the third chapter is a portrait of God's character where His true nature is represented: 'Then God saw their works, that they turned from their evil way; and God relented from the disaster that He had said He would bring upon them, and He did not do it' (3:10). Some people find it difficult to understand how God can threaten destruction; relent and still be an immutable God. Has God changed His mind? Has the action of the Ninevites dissuaded God from following through on His intended plan? No. God's threats of punishment have been, are, and will continue to be fulfilled with regard to those who habitually continue in their sin, refuse to repent and reject His offer of forgiveness, grace and mercy. God holds forth judgement in one hand and mercy in the other and it is up to people to decide to avail of the offer of mercy or not. The punishment depends upon the scorning of mercy in favour of sin; and mercy is contingent upon repentance; as Jonah said, "Those who regard worthless idols forsake their own mercy" (2:8). Or as the N.I.V. puts it, 'Those who cling to worthless idols forfeit the grace that could be theirs'.

God knew that Nineveh's response to His warning was genuine. It was not merely an outward ritual observed as a safe bet in averting any possible disaster. It was not merely formal or fearful obedience to their king's decree. God saw their inner and external transformation and He had compassion on them.

God responded to the attitude and action of the people and the proclamation of the king who said: "Who can tell *if* God will turn and relent, and turn away from His fierce anger, so that we may not perish?" (3:9). God observes the sincere desire of the Ninevites to put things right by giving up their evil ways and violence. The only conclusion we can possibly draw from this is that God accepted their repentance as genuine. The question; can God relent and still be an unchanging God, implies that if God changes His mind He is inconsistent. But God does not change His mind. Scripture occasionally speaks of God relenting or 'repenting' of decisions. All that has changed in these circumstances, such as Nineveh, is people's behaviour. God would have been inconsistent with His own nature if His threat of destruction was not removed in the light of the swift and sincere repentance of the Ninevites. God is conducting Himself in a completely consistent manner because His threats of judgement are conditional.

In Jeremiah 18 we can read God's own commentary on this issue:

> "The instant I speak concerning a nation and concerning a kingdom, to pluck up, to pull down, and to destroy *it,* if that nation against whom I have spoken turns from its evil, I will relent of the disaster that I thought to bring upon it. And the instant I speak concerning a nation and concerning a kingdom, to build and to plant *it,* if it does evil in My sight so that it does not obey My voice, then I will relent concerning the good with which I said I would benefit it (7-10).

God's warnings are qualified and provisional warnings. These verses in Jeremiah explain God's consistency in His dealings with people. If people persist in their sin He will judge them but if they repent He will forgive. If the Ninevites had repented and God still judged them, He would be breaching His own transparent policy and procedure in dealing with sinners. The people are not the authors of their own salvation through their repentance rather they are availing of the mercy of God which is accessible by genuine contrition.

The event of the cross cannot be reduced to an astonishing manifestation of love because it is more than that. There is no salvation available to anybody merely because they repent. When we repent our past has to be dealt with. Even if we resolve never to sin again and succeed in that resolution (which I believe is not possible) the past must be purged. At Calvary God poured out the awful but righteous anger, that we deserved, unto His beloved, perfect and only Son. There must be a change in our hearts but there has to be a corresponding change in the heart of God. This does not render God indecisive or inconsistent rather it shows Him as totally constant and unwavering in relation to His Word.

Many people think the idea that God would destroy a city, nation or kingdom is disgusting. The prevailing secular mindset finds the very notion of punishment disagreeable. Modern prisons in Western[30] society are essentially rehabilitative rather than retributive. The deprivation of a person's liberty is regarded as sufficient penalty for serious crimes. So the idea that God would chastise people and punish wickedness is disagreeable to the contemporary mind. Much of Scripture is unpleasant and disagreeable to the so called, contemporary, 'progressive' and 'enlightened' mind. Political correctness censors and censures a Christian worldview with regard to our origin and purpose and also our destiny in the afterlife. We cannot speak of creation without being ridiculed. We cannot speak of the sanctity of life in abortion debates or euthanasia debates without incurring the wrath of evangelistic unbelievers who preach a 'gospel' of atheism. We cannot speak of hell without stirring up that inherent anti-religious sentiment. There is

---

[30] Except, prisons in some states of the USA, where the death penalty is enforced. Statistics show that homicides are highest in states where the death penalty is imposed. This shows that it is in itself an ineffective deterrent to murder and is clearly a punitive measure. One could argue that without the death penalty on the statute books of such states the numbers of homicides would be even higher but this others would say that this is a spurious argument that is not credible.

a predisposed antipathy to the things of God and to truth. The Christian feels he is walking on thin ice because there is this code of political correctness. But as believers we should be more interested in biblical correctness than political correctness.

Should we understand the repentance of the Ninevites on the occasion of Jonah's preaching as a lasting spiritual redemption? It is, perhaps, better understood as a temporal deliverance from total destruction. God's wrath was averted and in this sense it was a terrestrial redemption rather than a celestial salvation. This event cannot be seen as the conversion of Nineveh's inhabitants to Judaism. It cannot be interpreted rightly in that way, although it is frequently used in such a manner in preaching and teaching. Their repentance was sufficiently genuine that God did not bring disaster upon them at that time. It is possible that in that generation, many, some or all of them followed God for a time. We cannot say for certain what kind of lasting effect the Word of God had upon them. We know that their destruction was temporarily averted at the time of Jonah. However, approximately a century after Nineveh's contrition, authentic as it was at the time, Nineveh had gone back to its wicked ways with renewed intensity and had, as part of an Assyrian onslaught, annihilated the northern kingdom of Israel. Nahum's ministry was to bring comfort to God's people in the southern kingdom of Judah by announcing judgement against Nineveh.

Nahum prophesied Nineveh's fall which was fulfilled in 612 B.C. The theme and message of Nahum essentially focuses on God's judgement on Nineveh for its oppression, cruelty, idolatry and wickedness. It shows that God's righteous and just kingdom will eventually prevail because kingdoms built on wickedness and tyranny must eventually fall, as Assyria did. In this we see that God is the Lord of history and of all the nations of the world, and they are subject to His sovereign control. God is aware of the evil that exists in the world and He will destroy those who are vicious and mercilessness advocates and defenders of brutality.

In Nahum we see that God upholds justice and comforts and champions His people. We learn from this that God wants His people to uphold justice and fairness in all their dealings with others; personal; corporate; business; national and international relations. This is a crucially important message.

When so-called Christian leaders fail to condemn violence or are slow to do it they are rightly perceived as reluctant to promote fairness and justice. As Western Christians have we presided over inequitable political and socio-economic structures and perpetuated the political status quo in situations that are morally wrong?

Jonah is a message for our generation but sometimes Christians cannot fathom it. Christians can be religiously prejudiced and politically partisan. In some traditions patriotism and religion merge into a synthesis that is fanatical and frightening. Jonah had much to learn about the merciful nature and gracious heart of God and so do we, irrespective of our culture and traditions.

When God sent another message to Nineveh through the prophet Nahum it was a scathing denunciation of their sinfulness. This time they were destroyed and to this day Nineveh has never been rebuilt. Nahum declares the universal sovereignty of God in determining the destinies of nations.

Jonah's mission was to demonstrate that God was a universal God who extended grace, not only to the Israelites, but to all nations, even the wicked Ninevites of Assyria. What we need to learn from this is that God loves humanity and wants everybody to hear the gospel. We also learn that it is impossible to hide from God because He sees everything and knows everything. If we rebel against God's will He will permit us to go through a set of circumstances and experiences which are painful and purposeful in drawing us back to His will. He gives us a second chance to serve Him honourably. Jonah had much to learn about the gracious heart of God. In sending Jonah to Nineveh God was demonstrating the fact that He is a universal God. He has an interest in nations other than Israel and He has an interest today in peoples who are not Christian.

In Matthew 12 Jesus refers to 'the preaching of Jonah' (v.41). Preaching is a discourse where the preacher delivers an address to people, which involves urging and exhortation. Preaching is God's ordained means of revealing Himself and illuminating His redemptive purposes. Evangelistic preaching is God's self-disclosure, through His Word, which is apprehended by a response of faith expressed in repentance. Jonah's preaching was effective because it was God's Word, boldly delivered and clearly and accurately explained. The efficacy of the preached word depends primarily on the content of the message rather than the carrier of that communication. This is evident in the preaching of this reluctant prophet.

It is doubtful that Jonah went about Nineveh merely repeating, "Yet forty days, and Nineveh shall be overthrown!" In 1:2 The Lord told Jonah, "Arise, go to Nineveh, that great city, and cry out against it; for their wickedness has come up before Me." In 3:2 the Lord told Jonah to "Arise, go to Nineveh, that great city, and preach to it the message that I tell you." So Jonah was instructed to "preach to it" because its wickedness was an offence to God. Clearly Jonah is charged with the task of condemning the wickedness of Nineveh in the name of the Lord. He is told the reason why he is to preach and he is directed by God not only about the cause of God's wrath but also the content of God's Word.

The response of the people indicates that they understood there was a possibility of escaping judgement.

Their action demonstrates that they hoped to avert the anger of the Almighty. They did not, as stated earlier, take Jonah's words as the inexorable destiny of Nineveh and its inhabitants. They did not flee the city in the hope of escaping an inevitable destruction of that place and its population. They did not respond by saying, we have just about six more weeks to continue to live and behave as we have always done and redouble their evil. They did not decide to flay Jonah alive and scoff at him or his message.

Somehow the possibility of appeasing God became the popular reaction and this is partly explained by the probability that Jonah preached repentance as well as judgement. However, it can only be fully explained by recognising that God's Word brought about a conviction of sin and a corresponding confession of their wickedness that averted their ruin. But that is not a complete explanation either. It must be understood that it was not exclusively the fact that they had turned from their evil ways that brought about their escaping judgement; rather it was the gracious and merciful response of God. God had compassion (3:10). God has compassion for wicked, heathen people. Today that same God has that same compassion for the hedonistic, homosexual, heterosexual, permissive and violent people of our generation.

People may be indifferent, antagonistic or accepting of the Word given by God through His commissioned servants. The awesome reality of anointed expository preaching is that it stimulates repentance and strengthens faith. It may also stir up rebellion and rejection of the Word which ends in judgement. Salvation comes through the hearing of the Word of God. To suspend the preaching of Scripture and prefer anecdotal, entertaining and sensational substitutes is a grievous mistake that some contemporary churches have made. The Word of God discloses the mind of God and the condition of mankind. If it is displaced churches may increase numerically but decrease in the number of people who have knowledge of God as Saviour. Preaching is the doorway to the eternal destiny of souls. To amuse people and preach only what is popular may produce larger congregations of people who are never seriously challenged on matters of spiritual importance. Some mega-churches have conducted surveys to ascertain what of other faiths people would prefer church to be. Then they set up a church that is focused on what their expectations and preferences would be.

People's needs are important but their most crucial need, whether they know it or not, is to come to faith in Christ through repentance of sin. The cross must be central and every text and theme sprinkled or drenched in the blood of Christ. If we deprive people of this we are guilty of hiding the way to heaven. There is a critical need in our generation for *fearless* and *faithful* preachers. There is a plentiful quantity of diplomatic pastors but there is a scarcity of quality preachers. These cautious preachers prefer to court friendliness and calculate it to be of more crucial importance than proclaiming the whole counsel of God without fear or favour. Person-pleasers will not uphold truth for fear of alienating people who might dislike its emphasis and implications.

People need preaching embedded in Scripture, germane to our generation anointed by God and delivered with conviction by men unreservedly and unashamedly committed to the Word of God. The message of the gospel is unpalatable to many. Today there is an emphasis on dramatic performances, music, power-point presentations and modern methods. These things are not necessarily or inherently inappropriate. It is the obsession with them and the devaluation of preaching as a consequence that is the problem. Where dialogue is preferred to didactic teaching or 'doctrinaire' preaching the church will be shallow not solid. Churches that downgrade preaching are destitute and deceived into thinking they are successful. They may be reaching people but with what; novelty? The strength of the church is that all its activities are rooted in the Word of God.

Jesus said: "The men of Nineveh will stand up at the judgement with this generation and condemn it; for they repented at the preaching of Jonah, and now one greater than Jonah is here" (Mt.12:41). The words of Jesus about the men of Nineveh will certainly apply to Christ's earthly contemporaries but will it apply to subsequent generations, including our own? We live post-Calvary with the benefit of almost three-thousand years more revelation than the Ninevites and two thousand years after Christ's generation. The critical question is this; are we, in our generation, preaching the impending judgement of unrepentant sinners and the opportunity of mercy and grace for the penitent? If we are going to lead people to faith, and maturity we must preach the Word that God has given in all its power and prophetic potency.

8.

Spiritual Signs

An important issue which needs some attention is 'the sign of Jonah'. This is critical to any analysis of the Old Testament prophetic book. Matthew 12:38-45 records Jesus speaking about, 'The Sign of Jonah'. Here the Saviour speaks of the life and testimony of the Old Testament prophet. Liberal theology presents *Jonah* as a parable. Yet it is clear from the words of Christ that Jesus believed in the historical reality of the events recorded in *Jonah*. Scholars who portray *Jonah* as merely a story used to illustrate a moral or spiritual lesson contradict Christ. We are presented, therefore with a choice of interpretation.

Firstly, we can believe the liberal scholars. The implication of doing this, however, is that we decide to disagree with Christ. On what basis do we contradict Jesus? If we prefer to accept the liberal theological opinion we are effectively saying that Christ was merely a man of His generation and believed the fable like other uneducated and superstitious people of His time. We are saying that *Jonah* was merely part of their folklore, an allegory that taught some important lessons and principles.

Secondly, we can decide to believe in the historicity of *Jonah* because Jesus believed it. In this passage Jesus uses the experience of Jonah to predict His own burial. If *Jonah* was no more than a moral tale it would be a rather inappropriate story to use in association with predicting His own resurrection. In fact Christ uses the reference to

Jonah as one of several historical people. He refers to 'the men of Nineveh', 'The Queen of the South' (a reference to the Queen of Sheba), 'Solomon' and Himself as 'a greater than Solomon'; the promised Messiah. The fact that these other characters are plainly historical confirms the historical reality of Jonah. It would be most improbable that the Lord would include a mythical figure (as some liberal scholars see Jonah) in the same context as these other historical individuals.

The choice comes down to believing Jesus or the theories of men. If Jesus was wrong about *Jonah* how could anything else that He said have any credibility? Jesus chose to refer to Jonah in predicting the central truth of the Christian faith; His resurrection. To base such a crucial event on a mythical figure would have been foolish. But in all encounters with Christ throughout the gospels Jesus is portrayed as profoundly wise. He outsmarted the Pharisees who often sought to trap Him. His teaching was/is so amazingly insightful that to attribute foolishness to His words would merely expose those who question His standing on *Jonah* as unwise.

Jesus teaching on 'The Sign of Jonah' was very relevant in his generation and is also pertinent in our day. The Pharisees were present when Jesus spoke of this and it is important that we pay some attention to the background and context in which the Pharisees and teachers of the law asked (or perhaps demanded, as they and the Sadducees did in Mt.16) a miraculous sign. In the scene immediately preceding the passage that refers to, 'The Sign of Jonah', people bring a demon possessed man who is blind and mute to Jesus and the Lord healed him so that he could both talk and see. The people were amazed and wondered if Jesus was the Messiah. This outraged the Pharisees who accused Him of being in league with Beelzebub (the Devil), the prince of demons. Jesus exposes the stupidity of their argument in His reply and issues a sharp warning to them to be careful what they say about the Christ. He calls them a brood of vipers and tells them, "But I say to you that for every idle word men may speak, they will give account of it in the day of judgment" (Mt.12:36). Prior to this the Pharisees complained about Christ's disciples picking heads of grain and eating them on the Sabbath. These people wanted to trip Jesus up. There was no sincerity in their questions.

If we go back to Matthew 11:20-25 this is a passage where Jesus denounced the unrepentant cities in which most of His miracles were performed. He did this because of their unbelief and refusal to repent in spite of many signs and wonders performed before them. He condemns places such as Korazin, Bethsaida saying that if such miracles had been performed in Tyre and Sidon they would have "repented long ago in sackcloth and ashes" (vs.21-22). With regard to the miracles performed in Capernaum Jesus said that if the miracles performed there had been performed in Sodom "it would have remained until this day" (v.23).

So when we come to the passage known as 'The Sign of Jonah' (Mt.12:38-45) where Jesus replies to the Pharisees demand to see a miraculous sign we have already learned that Jesus knew that miraculous signs did not necessarily bring repentance and that the Pharisees were insincere in their questions. Thus we read: 'But He answered and said to them, "An evil and adulterous generation seeks after a sign, and no sign will be given to it except the sign of the prophet Jonah" ' (v.39).

A common Jewish way of reckoning would have included at least part of the first day and part of the third day to count as three days. The Pharisees wanted to see a spectacular miracle but Jesus refers to a historical sign instead. Two important issues emerge from this.

Firstly, eagerness for the sensational is not a sign of spiritual maturity. In fact Jesus makes it known that such a curiosity is immature or even perverse. In Christianity today there is a desire for the sensational, the miraculous and the dramatic. People are attracted to churches that have entertaining performances. They like to be amused and to have something novel and emotionally stimulating. But people who desire and expect this as a prerequisite to believing are, according to Jesus, evil, adulterous and immature.

Secondly, we will be judged on the basis of the revelation that we have received. God is supernatural, He can and does demonstrate His miraculous power. He can do astonishing and magnificent things. Nevertheless this is not the normal way God works. All Christians should believe in the miraculous power of God. Every birth and every second (spiritual) birth is proof that God is a God of the miraculous. God still does amazing and dramatic things but this is not His usual way of working. At special times and in specific places God has done dramatic things to attract people to Jesus. Among un-reached people who have no knowledge of the Word of God and no framework in which to set biblical truth, missionaries have reported miraculous incidents. On special occasions in some remote jungles of the world where evangelists did not know the local dialect, the Holy Spirit opened the mouths of the messengers and the ears of the tribes-people so that the gospel could be, miraculously, communicated. We cannot say that God cannot do sensational things today. But we can say that this is not God's modus operandi.

The problem of the people of Christ's generation was that they had the revealed Old Testament Scriptures. This is also the difficulty in our day. We have the revealed Word of God. It is through Scripture that God communicates today. It is the normal and normative way in which God speaks to His people and to those who are being wooed by His overtures of mercy and grace. In the passage, 'The Sign of Jonah', Jesus effectively says, "you don't need signs and wonders and spectacular miracles because the Messiah, the Christ, Jesus is with you." Jesus was saying, look to Me, not for sensational events and drama. He is reprimanding them by saying that they are in the very presence of the Messiah and they are seeking something other than Him, some thrilling event.

Today we have the Scriptures and they tell us everything we need to know for salvation and sanctification too. So to look for more; to be unsatisfied with anything less than some breathtaking melodramatic experience is an indication of spiritual immaturity. To desire or demand more is a sign of scepticism rather than faith. Christians should learn to be content with the treasure of Scripture. This is where we find the Saviour and the means of sanctification. This is where we find guidance and direction. This is where we find comfort and solace. This is where we learn to know more of God. This is where He becomes intimate with us and it is also where He moulds us into the image of His Son.

Jesus told these Pharisees that the only supernatural sign they would receive would be His resurrection which He likened to Jonah being three days and three nights in the belly of the great fish. We know from the gospel accounts how sceptical they were regarding reports of that fact and how cynical and critical they became about those who claimed Jesus had risen from the dead.

'The sign of Jonah' was both a *visible* and *verbal* sign. The reappearance of Jonah after three days in the belly of the great fish meant that the man was himself, a message. Before he uttered a word about God's impending judgement, his very appearance, which likely required some explaining, spoke of a God who forgives and spares the repentant. Jonah was a visual aid that demonstrated these qualities of God. News of this strange man arriving in Nineveh probably spread rapidly among the people.

9.

Missionary Mindset

Chapter 3 ends with the marvellous theme of God's mercy. It is not possible for mortals to fully comprehend this attribute of the Almighty. If the story had ended there the book of *Jonah* would be entirely different than it is. So far it has dealt with Jonah's commissioning, his rebellion, chastisement, repentance, rescue, re-commissioning and obedience. The mission to Nineveh is a tremendous success. God's inclination toward mercy rather than judgement is established and the Assyrian people are spared the destruction they deserved. But the message of *Jonah* is not yet complete. In chapter 4 the reason for the prophet's obstinate attitude and action in running away initially comes to light. It is difficult for the Christian today to understand such a man and his mindset. Any missionary today would be thrilled with such an outcome and would rightly rejoice in the salvation of so many souls. In chapter 4, however, we meet the pouting prophet and his response to God's sovereign right to be merciful to whomsoever He wishes. He is both puzzling and perplexing.

God is now demonstrating mercy to this rather mystifying preacher. Here is an interesting portrait of God's patience with His people. He deals with Jonah as He often deals with His children, in an intimate and affectionate manner. Even though Jonah's demeanour is provocative and could rightly warrant the wrath of God, yet the Lord is patient with him. Such tolerant and tender dealing with the prophet is typical of God, who is forbearing and forgiving of human finitude in understanding the charitable heart and mind of the Almighty.

There is a concept in group facilitation skills which is known as, 'warm authority'. Essentially this means that the facilitator can control any member of the group without damaging the dignity of the individual. Some people have a natural flair for this, whereas others work at it. I have known pastors who have this gift; men who are not afraid to challenge wrong attitudes expressed in the home-Bible-study group, while retaining the respect of the person being gently reprimanded. When we consider how God speaks to Jonah in chapter 4 we are witnessing the supreme example of 'warm authority'.

Jonah's courage in proclaiming the Word of the Lord in Nineveh showed some degree of character which is now compromised by his anger and failure to accept the will of God. Jonah understood the nature of God and the outcome of his preaching was not unexpected. The attitude of Jonah is like that of a petulant child who is frustrated by the will of a parent. The opening verse of chapter 4 says that 'it displeased Jonah exceedingly, and he became angry' and this is a stark contrast with the closing verse of chapter 3 which says: 'Then God saw their works, that they turned from their evil way; and God relented from the disaster that He had said He would bring upon them, and He did not do it' (v.10). It is not an accidental or incidental detail of the narrative that these very different attributes are put side by side. This arrangement in the text would have immediately confronted and challenged Hebrew exclusivist assumptions. They had come to think of themselves not as champions of truth but as the custodians and sole beneficiaries of God's bountiful blessings. They had misinterpreted the covenant intentions of God who promised that through Israel all nations would be blessed.

Jonah knew that God was merciful and his attitude reveals a disregard for God's will. He would rather pray the Ninevites were destroyed. This is a shocking indictment of a man of God who has the cheek to pray: "Ah, LORD, was not this what I said when I was still in my country? Therefore I fled previously to Tarshish; for I know that You *are* a gracious and merciful God, slow to anger and abundant in lovingkindness, One who relents from doing harm" (4:2). This is consistent with God's self-disclosure of His true nature to Moses (Ex.34:6). The preacher's attitude is reminiscent of Jeremiah's complaint:

> O LORD, You induced me, and I was persuaded;
> You are stronger than I, and have prevailed.
> I am in derision daily;
> Everyone mocks me.
> For when I spoke, I cried out;
> I shouted, "Violence and plunder!"
> Because the word of the LORD was made to me
> A reproach and a derision daily (Jer.20:7-8).

Jonah was prejudiced against the Ninevites and did not want to be instrumental in extending God's mercy to these heathen enemies of Israel. He saw them as a potential threat to the security of Israel and a contaminating influence on the purity of the covenant as he understood it. In this attitude he totally misrepresents the Lord. He did not want God to be benevolent in dispensing grace. His theology constrained and circumscribed God's blessing to the circumcised of Israel.[31] He would rather pray God reserved His grace for those within the borders of his nation. He was nationalistic and some might think he should be commended rather than condemned for his patriotism. I

---

[31] This would not exclude women. Although female circumcision was not practiced by the Hebrews, a circumcision of the heart would include females. The physical circumcision of males was merely a sign or mark of covenant belonging.

do not condemn him, he was a victim of his culture and loyal to his traditions. We all need to examine our preconceptions and misconceptions in the light of God's Word.

The message of *Jonah* in this fourth chapter is relevant today. There are exclusivist attitudes that need to be changed. There are straight-jacketed preachers who are hesitant to preach grace because their theological traditions are controlled by theories about God that misinterpret His true nature, which is essentially and primarily compassionate. They misrepresent Him because they prefer their theology to the truth. A preacher who is tentative in proclaiming God's grace is an ornamental rather than an instrumental vessel of God. God is not swift to condemn. God delays destruction and delights in grace. I am not suggesting that a preacher should preach grace only. But I do suggest that a preacher should preach grace always. In other words, messages about judgement should be seasoned with grace. Hell should be preached in the context of heaven. Rebuke should be tempered with tenderness. The preacher who reprimands and reproaches without reference to grace is representing a scolding father who is sparse and meagre in saving and sanctifying mercy. God is rich in love and copiously compassionate. God grants grace extravagantly. God is bountiful with blessing. God is not begrudging in grace and He delights greatly to multiply mercy, to lavish love and to give grace.

So Jonah was prejudiced. Is that what God is saying in this Old Testament book? Yes, and no! It is interesting to note that Jonah was prejudiced but it is more instructive to discern what God is saying to the present generation in this timeless message of mercy. God does not want Christians to merely scrutinise this book for a better understanding of an ancient prophet's attitude. God does not want us to explore His attributes in a merely academic manner. Rather He wants us to examine our lives in the light of this revelation of His merciful nature and conform to His way of thinking. This is the process that Christians call 'the renewing of our minds'. It is a delight to see mercy manifest in the secular world but it is a sacred virtue of God that is part of His manifold essence. It is, therefore, sad and disturbing when that aspect of God's love is absent amongst those who claim to be disciples of Jesus. God wants us to examine ourselves in the light of this truth and represent Him as faithful ambassadors of mercy. Rather than repressing the teaching of this book Christians should search out its profitability for portraying God in all His glorious grace. Doctrine, such as the 'Doctrine of God' must be based on God's self-disclosure of His nature and our daily lives should reflect His mercy. God has other attributes, such as holiness which means He has the sovereign right to judge and punish sin. Preachers who have not meditated upon God's mercy tend to overemphasise other qualities of His divine nature. God is then misrepresented as harsh and austere.

Jonah has been instrumental in an event of repentance on a large scale. This is the kind of response a preacher desires and prays about. Readers of this book might expect Jonah to be delighted but find instead that he is dejected. It is difficult to fathom but the reality was that Jonah was greatly displeased and became angry. If this story finished at the end of chapter 3 Jonah's reputation would be very different today. Here is the other side of the coin in Jonah's flawed character, first there was his prejudice and now the flip side reveals pride in equal proportions.

The outcome of Jonah's mission is something that preachers should and would consider a dream come true. The message of judgement had been announced and there is a positive response by the people who sincerely repent. Jonah's ministry has been breathtakingly successful but he is furious. God forgives the citizens of Nineveh for their cruelty and wickedness so that their destruction is averted. Thousands of lives are spared judgement and the prophet has a fit of pique.

Jonah's displeasure and anger are noted as well as his description of God's character. In his rage he reveals the real reason for his flight to Tarshish. He was unwilling to fulfil the commission God entrusted to him, not only because he despised and detested the Assyrians but also because he knew God could spare these people. For Jonah the thought that he would prophesy judgement and that the outcome would be salvation was a prospect he feared. This, he thought, would damage his reputation. He was a proud and patriotic Jew and would like to have been credited with the destruction of Nineveh. This would have satisfied his appetite for avenging an enemy of Israel, noted for their brutality. He could return home to a heroes welcome.

It is possible, if not probable, that he entertained thoughts of the destruction of Nineveh because he wanted to be the champion of His people's cause. He wanted to be the one who would secure and strengthen Israel's position in the Middle-East. He loathed the idea of being seen as a failure; for predicting judgement and being instrumental in delivering salvation. He preferred his reputation above the lives of these men, women and children. A man's reputation in ministry or in any secular context is of immense value. Men will fight for their reputations. This is evident today in lawsuits where people take legal action to defend themselves against libel and defamation of character.

Jonah now considered his reputation to be in ruins. In his distorted view of reality he was defamed by God! He took his case to the highest court in heaven and dared to remonstrate with the Lord. His status would now be diminished. His good name as an accurate foreteller of future events would be damaged. He would be the one who prepared the way for Israel's future defeat at the hands of the Assyrians. In his pride he desired a different role and perhaps cherished the thought of being recorded in the annals of Israel's sacred and secular history as a person of strategic significance. He was in reality a person of strategic significance but his pride led him to have different expectations. Where would he rank now amongst his eminent prophetic predecessors? What kind of standing would he have now amongst his own people? How could he face them? Like many other people of God he found security and status in his role and reputation. His occupation as a respectable minister of the Lord meant more to him than the mind of God. This is a point worthy of further reflection by those in Christian ministry today. Where does the preacher find his security and status; in ministry and mission or in God Himself?

In today's world Jonah would not be considered to have liberal theological views. On the contrary, he would be categorised as a thoroughbred, orthodox, and conservative evangelical. In theological terms it is not his understanding of the doctrine of God that is faulty. Jonah's understanding of his missionary task was based on a biblical understanding of God. His theology had not tutored and shaped his soul in the likeness of God. His understanding of the Lord (4:2) is a classic covenantal, creedal confession of the character of God found in the Old Testament (Ex.34:6-7). There are many such references to God's essential nature in the Scripture.

The instance cited in Exodus occurred when Moses returned to Mount Sinai to obtain the new tablets of stone. God made His *name* and *nature* known (Ex.34:7). Jonah knew that God could either forgive wickedness, rebellion and sin or, as the latter half of verse seven makes plain, He could punish wickedness: "by no means clearing *the guilty*". The background and circumstances surrounding God's proclamation of His character in *Exodus* 34 are worthy of note as they supply a framework for a balanced understanding of the character of God. Moses had descended Mount Sinai with the original tablets of stone to find the Hebrews engaged in idolatry and shameless immorality centred in the worship of the golden calf which Aaron had crafted. God ultimately punished the people with a plague for their physical wantonness and spiritual depravity (Ex.32:35).

Following this judgement God reissued the commandments. This signified that the special relationship with His chosen people, although damaged, was not destroyed. The bond had not been broken. God delights in forgiveness, compassion and mercy.

Jonah knew God well but he diverged fundamentally from the character of God in his pride and prejudice. It was these defects that brought him into conflict with God and led to his quarrelsome prayer (4:2). This certainty about the nature of God as gracious and compassionate shows a true knowledge of God. Yet, at the same time it exposes a failure to integrate that information beyond intelligence so that it could become a character transforming power. He knew the Lord would prefer pardon to punishment. He anticipated that God might take pity on the people and relent from imposing judgement. He knew that the Lord was not quick to condemn. He knew that God was merciful to a degree beyond measure. Is that our perception of God? Is that perspective perfecting us in mercy and grace and love? The Lord has not changed. He is still a God who would prefer to rescue wicked cities rather than raze them to the ground and obliterate their occupants. He pities the needy and has compassion for sinners.

Jonah understood that if he went to this great city of the Assyrian people to preach the message of judgement they would have opportunity to repent. He knew that God could forgive them but he does not relish the idea. On a personal level he harboured pride and prejudice. These two aspects of his flawed character are inextricably linked. He is concerned about his reputation and about the liberation of these loathed Ninevites. Jonah's pride and prejudice prevented him from graciously accepting God's will. The prophet himself would not have extended mercy to such a brutal people. We should be thankful to God that it is His standards of justice and mercy that are meted out to sinners such as us. If we were to depend on even God's spokespersons, prophets and preachers, we would be frequently denied the measure of mercy that God alone may dispense.

The Prayers of Jonah

In chapter 2 Jonah prays from the belly of the fish. It has been stated earlier that this prayer is steeped in biblical language, particularly that of the Psalms. It is a prayer of repentance and a plea for deliverance. It shows that no matter how awful our circumstances appear to be that God is still in control and hears and answers prayer. Even in the darkest and most extraordinary place God may be found. In fact it was God who put him in this peculiar place of confinement in order to save him from death by drowning in the stormy sea. When Jonah asked the sailors to throw him overboard (1:12) he was in effect asking them to kill him. He expected death to be the outcome. Given time to reflect on this desire to die he changed his mind and prayed for another chance to live.

By contrast, however, in chapter 4, Jonah is in a morbid state of mind again and asks God to take away his life. Warren Wiersbe said: 'Jonah prayed his best prayer in the worst place...and he prayed his worst prayer in the best place.' His first prayer came from a broken and contrite spirit but his second prayer came from a bitter and contentious spirit.

He did not have a great deal of fondness for life, his own or the Ninevites. The prophet did not want to face life because his reputation, as he understood it, was in tatters. Here again he thought it preferable to die than to live. In a temper tantrum motivated by pride in his reputation before men rather than before God, he begs for death. His heart is so perversely prejudiced that he is dismayed by God's mercy. This attitude is quite shocking.

In our age of sophisticated telecommunications the world has become a global village. Images of the devastation wrought by earthquakes can be seen on news programmes in our living-rooms. Some time ago the heartbreaking scenes of death and destruction in Pakistan-controlled Kashmir conveyed the horror of death on such a scale. The Irish news reporter, Charlie Bird went to the scene immediately (as is normal for the world's media) where he happened to meet the world famous cricketer, Imran Khan, in the devastated market place area. Mr. Khan put the situation in context, explaining that as many as 100,000 people may have died in this situation. Buried beneath the rubble, the stench of decomposing bodies was, Charlie Bird said; 'overwhelming'.

It is almost impossible to understand that this is what Jonah wanted for Nineveh, that every man, woman and child would be slaughtered by an avenging, holy God. It is difficult to comprehend that the sense of despair he feels at this point arises out of an aversion to God's mercy. His pride is seriously hurt. It can be concluded from this that if the Lord had destroyed Nineveh Jonah would have felt a sense of elation and satisfaction. How utterly weird! He would have been proud of his role in what he would have understood to be a great achievement. He possessed the privileged prophetic office. It was a valued office and there is a sense in which it is right to have a proper sense of pride in ministry as a preacher, teacher or missionary for God. It is right to have a sense of self-respect but there is a danger that self-respect will take central place in the life of God's servants. When this happens, as it does, God is displaced from the heart of ministry where He alone must take the most important and prominent position. Jonah had had an overvalued opinion of his worth and importance and that took pride of place in his heart.

Nineveh is described several times, directly by God, as a 'great city'. In the final verse of the book God, speaking to Jonah, refers to that place: "Nineveh, that great city, in which are more than one hundred and twenty thousand persons". The population of Nineveh therefore was at least 120,000. The phrase "persons who cannot discern between their right hand and their left" is ambiguous but interesting. What does it mean, exactly? Nobody can say precisely what it is meant to convey because it is unclear. Does it mean that these Ninevites know nothing of God's ways because they are ignorant of the covenant law which gives direction? Does it mean that it has 120,000 very young children (or people of sub-normal intelligence) who have not learned to distinguish right from left? If it means 'children' then the population of Nineveh would have been substantially greater than 120,000, possibly about 2 million[32].

God also says that Nineveh has, "much livestock". This is not an insignificant statement. No biblical expression is unimportant. The fact that God is speaking directly to Jonah about the lives of cattle means that it has some meaning. The commandments provided a Sabbath rest even for animals. The Psalms clearly state that 'God loves all that he has made'. This refers back to the Genesis account of creation where it is evident that God created all life forms, human, animal and vegetable. He created the Israelites, the Ninevites, the cattle, the fish, the gourd, the sun, and the worm. Thus God is concerned about biological and ecological life. God is not indifferent to animal welfare. By contrast Jonah has no regard for either animal or human life, including his own life.[33]

Can we have the same kind of bias about the value of life? The way the media reports certain incidents involving the loss of life seems disproportionate and gives the impression that a Western life is worth more than African or Asian life. There is a danger that we, as Christians place a higher value on a Christian life than a Muslim life. There

---

[32] It could simply mean 120,000 unsaved adults.

[33] He would have had a great respect for Israelite life and welfare.

is a danger that a greater importance may be placed on an Israeli life than a Palestinian life. This kind of prejudice can exist.

The message of *Jonah* has political/religious resonance which applies to the contemporary world. The Ninevites were a violent and potentially destructive enemy of Israel. Jonah was proud of his religious/political identity. He was a pedigree and patriotic Hebrew. He was a man loyal to his co-religionist/co-political people and implacably opposed to seeing his enemies benefiting from any sacred/ secular blessing.

Christians need to see the contemporary parallels with the message of *Jonah*. God's people are not to be characterised by belligerence and intransigence. God still reaches out in mercy to people of different religions, colour, race, ethnicity and political loyalties. God reached out to the Assyrian enemy of Israel. God is not a tribal deity, He is a universal God.

Jonah's Anger

There are two ways of looking at prejudice; positively and negatively. The Christian should have a bias toward biblical truth. Where this bias is present truth is protected and promoted. Where such bias is absent problems develops. It is right to have a prejudice in favour of truth as revealed in Scripture. It is right to have a bias against tradition taking an equal or superior place to Scriptural authority. Partiality itself is not the problem but when it impairs our judgement and causes blatant bigotry it becomes harmful.

Near the end of the story Jonah again pleads for death. He tells God that it would be better for him to die than to live (4:8). He is wallowing in self-pity for the hardship he endures in the scorching heat. In today's terms Jonah might be called a cross-cultural missionary. Yet he detests the physical discomfort which he experiences. He is sometimes portrayed simplistically as sulking or in a bad mood. This may be excused in junior Sunday-School classes where children are told that he is grumpy. But as these children grow into adults their understanding of the response of Jonah should also mature. It is inappropriate to think that Jonah was merely in a sullen and gloomy mood and that we all have this experience on occasions of disappointment. Perhaps Jonah's feelings can be partly attributed to a morose irritability in temperament but his emotional reaction cannot be fully explained in such terms.

He is livid and contends with God. He has the audacity to assert his right to be angry with the Almighty. He contests God's discernment, and in his opinion, *error* in the administration of justice. He is in fact judging God in questioning and condemning God's mercy by expressing his utter disapproval.

Verse 5 says: 'So Jonah went out of the city and sat on the east side of the city. There he made himself a shelter and sat under it in the shade, till he might see what would become of the city'. He knew God's inclination toward mercy. He knew God to be lenient and yet he waits to see what will happen to Nineveh. Now that he has argued with the Lord he hangs around to see if his protest has been successful in persuading or influencing God to change His mind and destroy the city. He is consistently out of harmony with God's heart in his desire for judgement.

God's Answer

The sinful people of Nineveh responded to the threat of judgement by meeting God's conditions of repentance thus averting the sentence that would otherwise have been imposed. Jonah is exceedingly displeased and very angry with this outcome but God's response to Jonah is a marvellous manifestation of mercy. The Lord condescends to converse with him. On two occasions He questions Jonah (4:4, 9). He is probing the heart of the prophet with the searching question, "*Is it* right for you to be angry?" It seems that Jonah is prone to anger. He is furious that God spared the people of Nineveh and he is irate that God removed the plant, provided by God, which protected Jonah from the searing heat. This incisive question should cause Jonah to engage in examining his heart. When God asks Jonah if he has, a right to be angry about the vine, the prophet claims that he does have that right.

Perhaps the question did not penetrate the hard heart of Jonah or maybe it did pierce his heart and found anger at its core. In either case his response to God's questioning is inappropriate, even though it is an accurate reflection of his state of mind on that occasion. Obviously he misses the shade which the plant provided and is feeling the effects of the high temperature but he claims he is angry enough to die. This may seem melodramatic but he is in a desert region under the blazing sun.

These questions apply not only uniquely to Jonah but universally to all mankind, especially to those who profess faith in the sovereignty of God. Jonah asserts that he is entitled to feel as he does. However sincerely he may feel about that, there is, in fact, no justification for such emotions. Yet anger against God is perhaps more common among believers than we realise or care to admit. Atheists will never experience this mood against God but believers may wonder why they are subject to suffering and question God and even become angry with Him. No matter how they try to suppress that feeling it will rise to the surface. It may never be overtly expressed but it is felt.

Jonah has experienced God's mercy in his own life but he begrudges others that same mercy. At a surface level it may be bewildering for the reader of *Jonah* to comprehend how a servant of God can have such an attitude. But when his pride and prejudice are examined the prophet's behaviour is seen in a whole new light. However, there is always the danger in reading Scripture in a way that avoids contemporary application. We need to search our own hearts to see if pride and prejudice harbour there.

Jonah was preoccupied with himself and with the privileged status of Israel. Can we be like that? Are we self-centred and so focused on church activity for God's redeemed that we neglect the lost? Are we indifferent to their spiritual condition? Are we culture-blind? Do we feel there is no point in evangelising in such and such a place because people there are so wicked that they deserve judgement? Maybe we are repulsed by some groups of people in society because of their ungodly lifestyles and hostility toward the church. Do we suppose that they fall outside the circumference of God's mercy? We must understand that God's heart is merciful enough to envelop even the vilest sinners. When we count ourselves among that group (sinners) then we will appreciate what Jonah failed to accept.

If we think of wickedness as something that other people could be legitimately charged with while thinking of ourselves as more worthy of mercy then we have a serious misunderstanding of ourselves. Do you think that because you were born into a Christian home with godly parents and came to the Lord at a young age that God didn't need to stoop so very low for you? Do you imagine that you merited God's favour because you had only little sins and had never been drunk, idolatrous, blasphemous or violent? Once we start to think like that we allow pride to distort the meaning of God's mercy and prejudice to germinate in our hearts. If we cherish God's mercy to us and meditate upon it often then it will be a safeguard against pride and prejudice. It will keep our hearts soft and manifest itself in tenderness toward all. This will starve sectarianism of the nourishment it needs to survive and thrive.

This Old Testament book confronts the people of God in all generations to look at themselves in the mirror of Scripture and ask if they resemble God or Jonah. This interrogative engagement between God and the prophet, in chapter 4, calls on Jonah to examine and explain his way of thinking. His theology was deficient. Biblical theology will draw God's people closer to the heart of God where there is no meagreness in mercy.

Object Lesson

Jonah has difficulty accepting God's will so the Lord gives him an object lesson. Jonah had built himself a shelter and sat in its shade. This temporary structure must have been inadequate in some way because 'the LORD God prepared a plant and made it come up over Jonah, that it might be shade for his head to deliver him from his misery. So Jonah was very grateful for the plant' (4:6). Jonah is more concerned about his own comfort than he is about the lives of the Ninevites. Right throughout the book the sovereignty of God is evident; the Lord sent a great wind upon the sea which stirred up a violent storm. Then the Lord provided a great fish to swallow Jonah. Then the Lord commanded the fish to spew Jonah onto dry land. This object lesson reinforces that theme. God sent the prophet, provided the vine which gave welcome shade, provided the worm which chewed the vine so that it withered and God provided a scorching east wind. Jonah was exposed to the intense heat.

The vine provided actual alleviation from the physical discomfort and accompanying emotional distress he was experiencing. However, it may also be viewed as symbolising God's mercy. The Lord provides protection for His people which, shelters them from the full force of His anger. In Psalm 121:5-6 the psalmist talks about how the Lord watches over his people:

> The LORD *is* your keeper;
> The LORD *is* your shade at your right hand.
> The sun shall not strike you by day,
> Nor the moon by night.

Isaiah 4 speaks of the branch of the Lord and of a canopy that '*will be* a covering. And there will be a tabernacle for shade in the daytime from the heat, for a place of refuge, and for a shelter from storm and rain' (5-6). The vine God provided for the intransigent prophet is more than physical shade; it is also the shield of God's merciful protection. In spite of Jonah's attitude God is still gracious to him. God indicates that His benevolence towards Jonah is unmerited mercy. The Lord rebukes him: "You have had pity on the plant for which you have not labored, nor made it grow, which came up in a night and perished in a night" (4:10). God is not only emphasising His sovereign right to provide and remove protection but also stressing Jonah's misplaced care. The prophet cared more about his comfort than he did about the lives of the Ninevites and God challenges him about this. At a minimum this object lesson serves three purposes, which are relevant, not only to Jonah, but also to the people of God in all ages.

Firstly, there is no justification for Jonah's feeling as he does. He has no moral entitlement to determine what should happen to Nineveh or the vine. God asks him, "*Is it* right for you to be angry?" This is a rhetorical question to which the only right and proper answer is "no". God is the creator of all life including the people of Nineveh, the animals, the vine and the worm. Their welfare depends on Him alone. It is His prerogative to govern life and death. Whatever seems best to Him should be the desire of God's people. As Jesus taught His disciples to pray, "Your will be done on earth as *it is* in heaven" (Mt.6:10). God's will is not questioned, doubted, opposed or criticised in heaven and that is as it should be among His people on earth. The heathen sailors appear to have a better appreciation of this than God's own prophet (1:14). They acknowledge God's right to act as He pleases.

In this dialogue between God and Jonah God points out that Jonah has no right to grumble about the withering plant when he is not the author of its life in the first instance. There is a blatant contrast between the superficial and selfish concern of the prophet for his own wellbeing and the profound care of God for His creation. The first application of the object lesson, therefore, is that neither Jonah nor anybody else has the right to judge others. This is the exclusive privilege of God and we should be content that it is so.

Secondly, Jonah does not convey any sense of gratitude for the grace of God. God has been gracious to him in spite of the fact that he refused to obey the first commission. Jonah fled to Tarshish and opted for death by drowning rather than repentance but God graciously spared him. Jonah seems to be totally unsuited to cross-cultural evangelism as he is more preoccupied with the covenant privileges of Israel and his own personal comfort than he is about the salvation of sinners. He seems unmindful of the fact that he too has been a beneficiary of God's mercy. God, in conversing with Jonah is gracious. God did not thunderously proclaim His lesson to Jonah in monologue form. Rather God engaged him gently with incisive questions. God is kind and patient with Jonah. Jonah has experienced the discipline of a good and gracious God. Whatever hardship and discomfort he encountered was the result of his disobedience and administered by God for the prophet's own good. Jonah repented in the belly of the fish and knew what it was like to experience the mercy of God. He was forgiven. God could have forgiven him and yet denied him the opportunity of further service. But God graciously re-commissioned him to the same task. Jonah deserved to die but God spared him. Yet he does not want others, who also deserve death, to share that same mercy and forgiveness. This is the second application of God's object lesson; that those who have experienced God's forgiveness and forbearance should be mindful of it. Furthermore this should cause them to desire that other, equally unworthy people, should come to encounter that same mercy.

Thirdly, God's love extends to people and places which we might deem to be outside the remit of grace. We cannot be theologically orthodox and devout and at the same time devoid of mercy. This is a contradiction. Herein is the difference between the sanctimonious and the sacred. Here is a potent image of God's compassion. God says, 'should I not pity Nineveh, that great city?' The word 'pity' literally means 'to act with tears in one's eyes'. God is concerned and He is declaring His right to weep over His creatures.

Undoubtedly God was disgusted by their wickedness and loathed their violence. Yet His heart yearned for their redemption. This is exactly how God views the nations of the world today. In spite of their idolatry and other forms of evil He desires their repentance, with tears in His eyes.

Are we moved to tears when interceding for the lost? Do we cry for those within our immediate and extended family circles who are strangers to the grace of God?

Christ's earthly ministry is marked with compassion. He wept over Jerusalem because he was concerned about the eternal destiny of its inhabitants. Do we share this concern for the spiritual condition of people? If we are going to effectually pray for the lost in our families, our circle of friends, our nation and the wider world I believe we have got to do it with more sincerity, more tears, more compassion and more concern. We cannot compromise the unpalatable truth of the gospel but we can proclaim it with tenderness. It is by no means certain that Jonah ever actually learned these lessons but we are without excuse and must learn and apply the insights we glean from this astonishing book.

The Missionary Heart of God

Jonah teaches us much about the missionary heart of God. Many churches today view mission as a relatively unimportant optional extra in the life of the church. This is reflected in poor attendance at missionary prayer meetings and visiting missionaries are likely to get a low attendance. Missionary mindedness is seen as an antiquated eccentricity.

The book of *Jonah* teaches us a great deal about the tender heart of God. The Almighty has compassion for all the nations and peoples of this planet, irrespective of class, culture or creedal conviction. Jonah could not comprehend the idea that God's love and vision extended beyond the covenant community of Israel. He failed to understand God's purposes for Israel. Starting with Abram God chose a man, a family, a tribe, a clan and a nation so that they could bear witness of Him to all nations. But Israel had come to think of itself as the ultimate and final object of God's affections. But God's vision was and still is, global.

Bearing witness of God is often narrowly understood as proclaiming the message of the gospel. Many Christians seem to think that fidelity to the words of Scripture in accurately conveying the message is adequate but it is not. As ambassadors of Christ we have a duty to represent Him and we fall short of our duty if we do not convey something of the love, compassion and tenderness of His heart. Why is it that some people who profess the doctrine of grace as a central tenet of faith are themselves ungracious people. Christians are prone to believe that they have a monopoly on love, mercy and grace and that these qualities can only be fully understood and appreciated by them. Such believers, cocooned in evangelical enclaves, need to know that this idea is false. Christians *should* be the ones in this world who demonstrate these qualities of God in their lives but in reality the people of other faiths often exhibit more kindness, tenderness, grace, mercy and love. When Christians are hard, intransigent and unforgiving they do not bear the family resemblance to Christ.

God never intended that His mercy would be confined exclusively to Israel. Similarly God does not intend that His mercy should apply only to those in the church. Israel was to play a strategic role in the unfolding of redemptive history. Mercy and grace was commenced but not completed there. Likewise the church is to play a role in fulfilling God's purposes but it is not the only sphere in which God is active in this world. Some Christians seem to think that the church is an exclusive club for the pious[34]. God reaches out to the unqualified and unworthy and embraces them. When we are hardhearted we misrepresent God and we need to be very careful that the God we worship is not merely an idolatrous version of our distorted religious imaginations.

Jonah, however, was typical of his contemporary co-religionists in thinking that the privileges of God's grace were the sole prerogative of Israel. Jesus said, "And other sheep I have which are not of this fold; them also I must bring" (Jn.10:16). In the context he is speaking to Jewish religious leaders about non-Jews who would be included in God's redemptive purposes.

The missionary mandate is not limited to what we call 'the great commission' nor is it confined to the New Testament. One pastor told me that he sometimes found it difficult to locate texts for 'Missionary Sundays'. He thought there were a limited number of passages in Scripture suited to a missionary theme. This is not an uncommon way of thinking as many Christians assume there are just a few proof texts in the *Bible* which support the doctrine of mission. The doctrine of mission has a strong biblical foundation because Scripture is essentially a mission text. It reveals the missionary mind and heart of God. Mission is not so much what God says, rather mission is about who God is. So the ultimate reason for mission is established on the basis of God's character. It is here we find support for the missionary enterprise. There are Scriptures that give voice to the obligation of mission but the ultimate foundation for missionary activity is the very nature of God.

The message of *Jonah* is remarkably relevant today because there is reluctance on the part of God's people to

---

[34] Thankfully there are many churches that are not like this. Many churches are characterised by love and compassion.

take the gospel to distant or difficult places. Previous generations have made heroic sacrifices to enter the mission field. When a missionary left his native homeland it was with a certain knowledge that he would be overseas for many years and might not ever return. Such journeys often took weeks or perhaps months to complete. Correspondence between the mission field and home would take at least a couple of months to complete the circle. These were the days before flights, cheap air-fares, email, internet, mobile phones, laptop computers, air-conditioning, effective medications against tropical diseases and CNN and BBC World News on television. But the Christian people of our grand-parents generation knew more about what God was doing in the world in their day than we do in ours. More importantly, they cared more about what God was doing. It is a sad fact that many Christian people today have no interest in what is happing beyond the boundaries of their narrow horizons.

Jonah represents a people who are reluctant to enter hostile territory. A church devoid of missionary vision is vulnerable to collapse or decline. A minister once told me he could not get involved in mission because his church was so weak. What he failed to realise is that failure to be involved in mission weakens a church. He said he could not invite me to his church to speak on the theme of mission because his church had many asylum seekers and refugees from quite a wide variety of nations. I must have seemed puzzled because he continued to explain that these recent converts were struggling with the basics of the faith. He concluded that a congregation of this profile was not yet ready for a missionary focus. But missions should fit in to our understanding of 'the basics of the faith'. A church should have a missionary vision instilled by biblical leaders from its very conception. This is what we see in Acts in spite of multi-ethnic and multi-linguistic issues.

Like many of God's people today Jonah is more concerned with his own reputation and physical comfort than he is with the spiritual welfare of those who are strangers to grace. We do not want to be inconvenienced. The book of *Jonah* clearly shows that the greatest obstacle to be overcome in fulfilling the missionary mandate is not ferocious opposition from those outside the covenant of grace but rather the pride, prejudice and selfish indifference of God's people.

Do we have compassion for the people who live in the great cities of the world where there is so much wickedness and so little witness? Are we willing to put our ambitions and plans aside and go with the gospel? Are we willing to go outside our own communities and ethnic group? Are we willing to make serious sacrifices in our standard of living to help resource missionary activity? Will we set aside our comfort, our pride and our prejudices and go to the heart of darkness with the light of the gospel? The sincerity of our answer lies not in our words but in our deeds.

The book of *Jonah* teaches us much about the man who didn't want to go to Nineveh. It teaches us a great deal about the character of God and it also teaches us much about ourselves. The Word of God is a mirror in which we see ourselves reflected. We must, therefore, heed the warning of James about the danger of not attending to the flaws in our attitudes and actions which it exposes.

In the light of Jonah there may be issues regarding how we spend our money and time that need to be addressed. Can we acknowledge the instinctive self-centredness of our inclinations? Will we admit that we are primarily concerned about our own convenience and comfort and that this ultimately has the effect of keeping God subordinate in our lives? God did not adapt to Jonah's mindset. We cannot be certain if Jonah ever fully yielded to a godly perspective on this issue. However, we may be sure that God is still seeking to teach us what he endeavoured to teach Jonah several thousands of years ago. The message is as relevant today as it was then.

Scripture sometimes edifies us and other times it rebukes and challenges us. We can savour the grace of God in our lives and frequently meditate upon His great love. But let these contemplations draw us to remember those who brought us the message of the gospel. Then in turn let us be responsive to the challenges of facing an unfinished task in bringing the gospel to all nations. Are we complacent? We need to rediscover the priorities of God and make them ours. His concerns should be ours. *Jonah* is a book that draws us close to the heart of God. May we be changed more into His likeness by conforming to His compassionate character.

www.ingramcontent.com/pod-product-compliance
Lightning Source LLC
LaVergne TN
LVHW090000180726
843489LV00001B/301